is an excellent source of knowledge and wisdom for anyone
o grow personally and desires to build a team professionally.
s extensive experience guides you through proven strategies to
eople into extraordinary performers."

Nido Qubein Chairman, Great Harvest Bread Co
President, High Point College

want to know what the 'latest and greatest' is, or what we need
ng for our client's future growth, Bob Moore is the first subject
rt we turn to. He not only stays current with research related to
organization performance, but he also is often on the leading
s especially effective in translating those research findings into
oth on a 'big picture' level and in the context that fits the specific
working with."

Noreen H. Hodges, Director
St. Petersburg College Corporate Training Program

k delivers transcendent wisdom where it matters: Centuries
nists dreamed of transforming leaden metal into gold. This is
at Bob reveals now. He reveals simple alchemic actions that
rm ordinary people into extraordinary outcome producers. His
perceptions are an ideal match for 21st century organizational
nt challenges. It is my privilege to have mentored Bob. His
light, his dazzling wisdom were vividly clear to me years ago.
rare qualities are accessible to you."

Burt Dubin, President
Personal Achievement Institute

been a great ally, consultant, sounding board, and partner in
build our management development programs. He has provided
d advice that has been invaluable. Bob was there at the beginning
ning Coach, and 14 years later we're still tweaking it together. His
e, enthusiasm, and commitment make it a please to work with

Edwin J. Nolan, Former Senior Director,
Training and Development Eckerd Corporation

ii

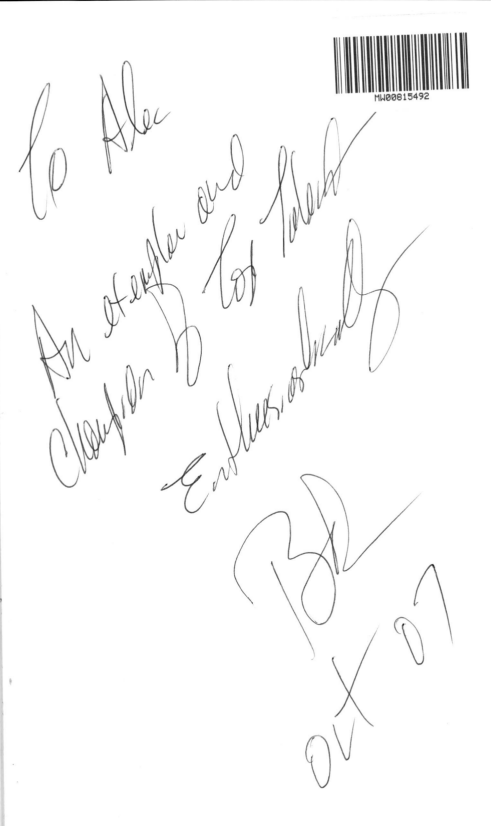

"Can you imagine the productivity if organizations implemented Bob Moore's wisdom and insights? Everyone would enjoy going to work, and the bottom line would be increased. The question is, are we willing to change?"

Joanna Weiland, CEO
Commanding View, Inc.

"As a mentor and friend for nearly fifteen years, Bob Moore has helped my clients and me reach new highs in top performance. With this latest book, Bob's wisdom is shared on a broader scale with anyone who truly aspires to make 'good' people be 'great'."

Dr. H. Joseph Marshall
Resource Management of Boston

"Bob Moore's book is a homerun! Read it and reap its piles of useful, relevant tips and ideas that will make you and your organization world class."

Bill Brooks, Author
The New Science of Sales and Persuasion

"Finally, someone has written a streetsmart book that can make a big difference in your organization. If you are serious about creating a culture of individual ownership, and accountability, this is a must-read book. And refer to it often, as it can be a catalyst for positive change!"

Mark LeBlanc
Author of *Growing Your Business!*

"Bob's book is most impressive. He has captured the pressing need to change the way we approach the development of organizations and personnel in this new era...I like the penetrating questions with which he challenges executives at the end of each chapter...I like everything about the book. This book should be in every MBA program."

Frank Edens PhD, Professor of Business,
Louisiana Tech University (retired)

"Bob Moore's book "Turning Good People Into Top Talent" is the right book at the right time for American business executives. It confronts head-on the principal challenges every "C" level executive faces in the New World Economy...A how-to kit on attracting, training, retaining and motivating top talent to consistently achieve the corporate vision and goals, this book is thought provoking, factual, solution-driven, timely, and full of real-world company examples. I recommend this book to all my consulting clients and friends."

John L. Nelson, President
Nelson Consulting, Inc.

"The biggest challenge most forward-thinking companies face in the next decade is the identification, development, and retention of top-performing people. The ideas presented in this book are pure gold. Study them, ingest them and, most importantly, put them to work for you...This book provides a blueprint for building a capability base that will carry your company to the next level and beyond."

George Morrisey, Author
***Morrisey on Planning* three-book series**

TURNING GOOD PEOPLE INTO

TOP TALENT

Key Leadership Strategies for a Winning Company

REVISED FOURTH EDITION

Bob Moore CMC, MCC

The Effectiveness Press

ISBN13: 978-0-9755623-3-8
ISBN: 0-9755623-3-9
Library of Congress Control Number: 2004111766

The Effectiveness Press books may be purchased for educational, business, or
sales promotional use. For information please write:

Special Markets Department

The Effectiveness Press

P. O. Box 25936, Tampa, FL 33622

inquiry@effectiveness.com www.toptalentbook.com

Cover and Interior Design by Amanda Finney,
Graphic Artist at Cameo Publications, LLC.

DEDICATION

To Mom (1919-2006), my champion for this project and my life.

ACKNOWLEDGEMENTS

Some of the many people who contributed to this book:

Nido Qubein, who offered to show me how a long time ago.

Roger Herman, who continuously nudged me to write a book.

Mark LeBlanc, who ignited the fire that finally got me going.

Ed Oakley, who gave me valuable mid course suggestions.

Stu Doyle, a dear friend and founder of my fan club.

Bertha and Ralph Morel, who were there when it mattered most.

Burt Dubin, who recognized my wisdom before I did.

Keith Ayers, a mentor and collaborator on vital elements found throughout the book.

Jeff Taylor, who pointed me forward with Positude®.

Bruce Magee, who gave me strategic unanticipated value.

John Butler, who encouraged me to cross the Rubicon.

John Nelson, for his guidance and acumen.

George Morrisey, a mentor and a guiding hand in pulling it all together.

My special colleagues in Coach University, Coachville, International Coach Federation, National Speakers Association, and fellow affiliates and business partners of Inscape Publishing, the Integro Leadership Institute, TTI Performance Systems, and others.

A few of my mentors whose impact is found within the pages of this book: Dave Buck, Bill Bonnstetter, Bill Brooks, Bill Cantrell, Don Cipriano, Carl George, Charlie "Tremendous" Jones, Thomas Leonard, Bill McGrane, Og Mandino, Anne Minton, Paul Mintz, Mike O'Connor, Bob Picha, Bob Pike, Cavett Robert, Jim Rohn, Dick Schultz, Steve Straus, Shayne Tracy, Stephen Tweed, Sandy Vilas, Ken Voges, Zig Ziglar, and the authors of the hundreds of books in my personal library.

Clients and project sponsors who have provided me with special opportunities to hone my craft and make this book possible: Bill Austin, Elsie Garner, Jim Heck, Noreen Hodges, Jim Kissane, Tracy Marple, Tommy Mayes, Ed Nolan, Mike Postlethwaite, James Wood, and Eric Jones.

TABLE OF CONTENTS

FOREWORD

In today's turbulent employment environment, Top Talent is at a premium. Good people are hard to find and even harder to keep. Employers who attract, optimize, and retain Top Talent will have a substantial competitive advantage.

For organizations to succeed, meet and exceed their objectives, and consistently stay at the top of their game, they must have effective leadership. If you're a leader in any kind of an organization, you would be well-advised to engage a Certified Management Consultant to work with your senior team and other people responsible for goal achievement.

Alternatively, you could bring in a Master Certified Coach who works with individuals to help them achieve their best performance. Bob Moore is both. With 30 years of experience in helping people and organizations become highly effective, he's an ideal choice to bring focus, energy, and technique to your team.

Now, in this advice-filled book, you can get Bob Moore in a small package. You'll learn from a down-to-earth consultant who's "been there, done that" and tells it like it is. He "talks" like a consultant, a coach, an advisor, and a friend. You'll feel like a favored client, learning about diagnosis, implementation, and getting results. Moore will challenge you to develop an action plan, to identify the principle concept you learned from each chapter, and to begin applying your new knowledge within 48 hours of learning it.

Yes, *Turning Good People into Top Talent* is an action-oriented tool. You'll even get assignments to complete to help you lock in the learning and jump-start your results.

- Roger Herman, CMC, CSP, FIMC
Author of the business best-seller, *Keeping Good People*

INTRODUCTION

Imagine . . . the positive impact on your bottom line with a workforce of fully engaged Top Talent executing your organization's strategy . . . every day!

A leadership strategy that includes talent management should be a top priority for executives of organizations focused on growth, customer satisfaction, and innovation. Effective talent management is essential to solve epidemic worker disengagement, high levels of employee turnover, and under-utilization of talent that limits competitive advantage.

Top Talent: Essential for Growth and Customer Satisfaction

Top Talent create the capacity for an organization to deliver the quality products, superior service, and exceptional value that result in customer loyalty, growth, and innovation. In his book *Good to Great*, Jim Collins reminds us that it is critical to get the right people on the bus and in the right seats...even before you decide where the bus is going.

Today, customers expect more value in everything they purchase, more of what they want than ever before. Many organizations appear content to deliver only expected value—exactly what the customer paid for and no more. This is characteristic of a transaction-based sale of a commodity with little or no value differentiation. Delivering expected value attracts price-shoppers.

The next level of value is achieved by providing customers with more than they expect, or value-added. Consistently providing value-added is a major step in building customer loyalty and differentiating yourself from price-based transactions.

17

Winning companies play a bigger game by providing unanticipated value. Consider the effect on customer loyalty when you provide your customers more value than they could have anticipated. An organization establishes itself as a strategic partner rather than a price-based commodity vendor by routinely delivering unanticipated value. Only Top Talent will have the capacity to consistently provide this level of value to your customers.

Top talent becomes essential to organizations as they shift their focus away from sales volume and product SKUs sold and toward customer-centric marketing that emphasizes building loyalty. Many retailers, particularly those in consumer electronics, such as Best Buy, are recognizing the importance of growing customer loyalty and increasing profit per customer by offering a one-stop, total solution for their most sophisticated buyers.

Don't Forget "The Good People"

Turning good people into Top Talent involves defining and assuring the fulfillment of the talent requirements of all essential positions from executives, managers, supervisors, and professionals to sales, customer service, production, and support.

Is it possible to hire Top Talent, to win the "War for Talent" on some recruiting battlefield? The fact is, people are not likely to be Top Talent when you hire them. Becoming Top Talent requires mastery of the essential skills for the particular job, a development process that is accomplished through effective talent management.

Most companies have good people—potential Top Talent—working away at their jobs, often unnoticed. In their book, *Winning*, Jack and Suzy Welch remind us that the typical organization has 20% top performers and 10% on the bottom. They emphasize the importance of recognizing the performance of the middle 70% who are the heart and soul—the central core—of the organization. Of particular importance are those in the top 20% of this central core—the valuable middle. If these workers are not properly recognized, they will leave in frustration for a place that appreciates them. This is the group I call "the good people" whom we can turn into top talent.

Nurturing Talent Pays Off Big

Rosenbluth International, the foremost travel management company since its industry's devastation following 9/11, has a 98% customer retention rate. With over $6.2 billion in annual sales, and profitability above industry standards, Rosenbluth has been recognized for Social Responsibility, Excellence in Communication, Exceptional Service, Corporate Culture/Leadership, and Industry-Specific Awards. CEO Hal Rosenbluth says, "Focusing on our people is the foundation. *Companies must put their people first.* Yes, even before their customers." This formula has worked for more than two decades and has transformed the company from a small family business founded by Rosenbluth's great-grandfather in 1892 into a global industry leader. The Rosenbluth story is a clear example that employees, not customers, should be management's top priority.

Talent Shortage

Many organizations are finding that there is just not enough talent to go around. Analysts expect more than 25% of the workforce to reach retirement by 2010, resulting in 10 million fewer employees than needed. The shortage of talented workers will become so severe within the next five years that those organizations with the ability to retain employees and maintain a stable workforce will have the competitive advantage. A young, talented workforce is critical to sustaining competitive advantage and accomplishing plans for growth.

The Herman Trend Alert Newsletter, written by Roger Herman, (www.hermangroup.com) has been predicting the talent shortage for several years and alerted us that retaining talent would become a serious issue.

Several surveys conducted in 2003 - 2004 revealed that 50 - 75% of workers surveyed said they would leave their present positions when the job market improved. With significant economic improvement, the percentage of workers who are unemployed because they quit is the highest since August 2001. Mark Zandi of Economy.com says, "People are feeling more confident about finding another job if they leave their current employment."

The Journey Ahead

Turning good people into Top Talent requires a road map and senior leadership commitment to implementation and follow-through. This is not a particularly difficult journey. However, it is new and different from what many organizations have been doing. Although leading an organization today is becoming increasingly complex, the principles in this book are easy-to-understand truths that many will find refreshing and inspiring.

While the following seven key leadership strategies for turning good people into Top Talent are presented sequentially, they are interdependent. I recommend prioritizing their application based on an objective diagnosis. For example, based on the survey described in Key Two, you may need to address one or more aspects of your organization's culture to create the climate for turning good people into Top Talent. Throughout the coming pages, you will be introduced to assessments and questionnaires including a readiness checklist discussed in Key One. Regardless of where you choose to begin, Key Seven, Talent Management, can be implemented immediately and become an ongoing process. I will cover this in more detail in the Review and Action Plan sections at the end.

Now, let's take a brief look at the Seven Key Leadership Strategies for Turning Good People Into Top Talent.

Key One – Accountability and a Responsibility-Based Workplace: Assuring Ownership and Commitment

Top performers who accept ownership and responsibility for achieving the accountabilities of their position require a trust-based environment. To accomplish this, leaders at all levels may need to learn how to release control and nurture responsibility among the work force.

Key Two – Organizational Vitality: Attracting and Energizing Top Talent

The more vitality an organization has, the more attractive it is to customers, employees, investors, suppliers, and other stakeholders. Begin by measuring your organization's vital signs such as alignment with vision, values, purpose, goals, procedures and roles, and the levels of trust and worker engagement.

Key Three – Shared Values: Assuring Credibility That Builds Trust

Core values by which the organization operates are critical to maintaining positive relationships with customers, employees and other stakeholders. Minimizing the gaps between the personal values people expect and what they experience enhances trust.

Key Four – High Performing Teams: Achieving Extraordinary Results

Creating high performing teams will allow achievement of the innovative breakthroughs that satisfy your customers. Achieving these results begins with an aligned senior team that models trust-building behaviors.

Key Five – Continuous Learning: Mastering the Essential Skills

Turning good people into Top Talent requires a continuous learning process that achieves mastery of the essential skills for the particular position. Begin by aligning all learning processes with the skills required to achieve the strategic accountabilities of the job.

Key Six – Coach-Based Management: Maximizing Worker and Manager Contribution

The most effective managers establish a coach-based employee-manager relationship. This includes mastery of emotional intelligence and people skills. Begin by assessing the leadership and management competency and skill levels at all levels within your organization.

Key Seven – Talent Management: Maximizing Engagement, Retention and Utilization

An effective talent management process includes identifying the talent requirements and benchmarking key positions essential to executing your strategy; implementing an effective hiring process to attract, screen, select, and bring on board good people who will become Top Talent.

Chapter Eight: Review and Action Plan

Winning companies have a strategy focused on achieving goals that include growth, customer satisfaction, and innovation. To execute a winning strategy, it is essential to include a talent management process that addresses epidemic worker disengagement, high levels of employee turnover, and under-utilization of talent.

Expect to be challenged to develop an action plan as you finish reading each section. By investing 25-30 minutes each day to read a section and complete the assignments, you can create a plan that will become key strategies for turning your good people into Top Talent. Let's get started on our journey.

Bob Moore
Tampa, Florida

KEY  ONE

ACCOUNTABILITY AND A RESPONSIBILITY-BASED WORKPLACE:

ASSURING OWNERSHIP AND COMMITMENT

> "The actions of managers obsessed with the bottom line have truly devastated the cultures of most large corporations. Making the workplace inviting to all employees—putting a meaningful human dimension back into it—is key to restoring an effective culture, which in turn is a proven way to guarantee long-term success."
>
> **- Allan Kennedy, *The End of Shareholder Value***

PART One

ACCOUNTABILITY AND A RESPONSIBILITY-BASED WORKPLACE:

Assertive Ownership and Commitment

ACCOUNTABILITY AND A RESPONSIBILITY-BASED WORKPLACE

A s organizations look for ways to increase productivity and profitability, accountability has become one of the most discussed and perplexing people-related issues. Managers frequently complain, "If only we could get our people to be accountable for results." Managers would like for workers to "just do it"—to get the job done right. At the same time, many workers want to be left alone to do the jobs they were hired to do. Accountability implies ownership, a condition based on an attitude that the individual can determine goals and objectives and the best way to achieve them. Workers must buy-in if they are expected to be personally responsible for the job's accountabilities.

The Need for a Compelling Vision

Many define vision as a mental picture of a future event as if it is already happening, seeing with the mind's eye what is possible in people, in projects, and in enterprises—especially your own. Having a compelling vision filled with imagery, sight, sound, feelings, taste, and smell attracts people much like a good restaurant does. Without a vision and a sense of hope, accepting reality may be discouraging. When effectively communicated, the vision enables everyone in the organization to focus his or her energies and resources. A compelling vision builds enthusiasm and acts as a catalyst for everyone to achieve the priorities.

Visionaries can be found everywhere, from the boardroom to the boiler room. Vision can be as focused as a clerk's vision of seeing files in perfect order, or it can be as broad as Coca-Cola's desire for everyone in the world to taste Coke. Walt Disney had a vision of a magical place that was fun for the whole family, which he then dramatically expressed by creating Disneyland. British poet, artist, print maker, and visionary William Blake once said, "What is now proved was once only imagined."

Visionaries know that the best way to predict the future is to create it. Instead of following the well-worn path, visionaries go where there is no path and blaze a new trail. Management philosopher Peter Koestenbaum tells us, "The visionary leader thinks big, thinks new, thinks ahead—and, most important, is in touch with the deep structure of human consciousness and creative potential."

Commitment to the Vision

How well people work together toward a shared vision increasingly determines organizational success. The most critical step to ensure the success of transforming your organization's culture to a responsibility-based workplace is to obtain everyone's commitment to achieving the organization's strategic vision or dream. What do you really want to achieve? What are the strategic reasons that make the commitment to this journey financially and emotionally worthwhile? Is the vision meaningful and compelling, something that all members of the senior team will buy into? Ask yourself, "What is possible if managers and employees work in partnership to create a great organization?"

Unless all key stakeholders agree to this strategic vision, the transformation process may fail when managers are asked to do things that make them uncomfortable—like being authentic and truthful with each other. If people begin to behave defensively, simply ask, "Is it really important to achieve (the strategic vision)? And can we achieve it without high levels of trust? Or without agreeing on the values by which we will operate?"

Back in 1991, before there was much talk about responsibility and accountability-based workplaces, Ed Oakley and Doug Krug, authors of *Enlightened Leadership*, observed that enlightened leaders have the ability to get the members of the organization to accept ownership for the vision as their own. This develops the commitment to carry it through to completion. Indeed, enlightened leaders nurture and encourage their people to be open, creative, and innovative, and to define what it takes to achieve their shared objectives.

Authority vs. Responsibility-Based Approaches

Managers may fear workers will choose to do less than the organization needs for them to do. Thus, they attempt to make workers responsible by holding them accountable. In fact, the opposite is true. Given a great place to work, employees will choose to produce far more than they would ever achieve when management attempts to force accountability.

I define accountability as taking personal responsibility for my behavior and work performance to achieve the agreed upon results. You can get your employees to be accountable for achieving results...willingly! Responsible employees already know they are accountable for producing results. They take ownership of their job, perform to the best of their ability, and continually look for ways to improve their performance. Top Talent places a high value on the opportunity to work where they can be responsible and accountable and have their work expectations met.

What kind of culture does it take to achieve the organization's vision? Table 1.1, based on the work of my associate Keith Ayers, president of the Integro Leadership Institute, compares cultural characteristics of an authority-driven workplace to those of a responsibility-based workplace. The key is to create an attractive workplace where people choose to be accountable. The most effective leaders understand that people willingly take personal responsibility for their performance and when they do, they will be accountable for results.

Authority vs. Responsibility	Authority-Driven Environment	Responsibility-Based Environment
Trust	Limited—How do you trust people who avoid responsibility, or have control over you?	Essential—Managers and employees focus on being trustworthy and building trust.
Leadership Behavior	Managers use rules, procedures, performance appraisals, and incentives to ensure compliance.	Leaders believe in people. They partner with employees to create a great organization.
Responsibility	No one wants to accept responsibility...stick to the rules and blame others for mistakes.	Everyone wants to be responsible, solve problems, and own the outcomes.
Employee Behavior Tendencies	Other-Directed people do what they're told, avoid taking risks, and use no initiative. Some rebel.	Self-Directed people are responsible and creative and use initiative. They take ownership of their jobs.

©**Integro Leadership Institute   Table 1.1**

Personal Responsibility

The following personal responsibility model from the Integro Leadership Institute Transforming Organizational Cultural Process™ illustrates the two paths a person tends to take, other-directed or self-directed.

	Other-Directed Authority-Based	*Self-Directed* Autonomy-Based
Belief:	"I have to"	"I choose to"
Attitude:	Comply or Rebel	Agree or Disagree
Reaction:	Resent or Resist	Accept Consequence
Feeling:	I am not responsible	I am responsible
Behavior:	Victim and/or revenge	Accountable

Following the self-directed approach, which is autonomy-based, individuals adopt a belief of "I choose to" and an attitude that they can agree or disagree. They accept the consequences of their choices because they feel responsible and behave with accountability.

Now let's follow the other-directed path, which is authority-based. Individuals react with either resentment or resistance and feel that they are not responsible. They behave like victims or seek revenge. These are the employees who tend to take long lunch breaks, come in late, and make personal calls or send emails on company time. Other-directed people tend to blame management when results fall short, since projects don't originate with them. They feel as if, "I never bought into it in the first place, so who cares?"

Which type of employee do you want on *your* payroll? Who is most likely to be fully engaged in doing what it takes to achieve the vision and purpose of the organization and in providing unanticipated value to your customers?

Ten Misguided Ideas

Beware of the trap that many leaders in corporate America have fallen into over the past 50 years in an attempt to get people to be accountable. In their book, *Accountability: Freedom and Responsibility Without Control*, Rob Lebow and Randy Spitzer present ten control-based approaches, misguided ideas that actually *prevent* people from being accountable:

1. Pay-for-performance and incentive programs

2. Internal competition

3. Performance reviews

4. Forced ranking systems

5. Personal improvement plans

6. Managing and supervising people

7. Restrictive policies and procedures

8. Employee recognition programs

9. Mission, vision, and values statements and slogans

10. Traditional job descriptions

How many of these approaches do you use in your organization? Before you begin to defend those you are using, ask yourself, "What is the real reason for implementing these practices?" If your answer has anything to do with an attempt to control or restrict, you are at great risk of producing a barrier to accountability. These ineffective techniques are flawed because they are based on a lack of trust that employees will make wise choices and use their time effectively. Ask yourself, "How long has it been since I examined my practices to determine if they are really effective?"

An Example of a Responsibility-Based Workplace

The concept of creating a responsibility-based workplace where employees are willing to own their jobs and to be accountable for personal performance is not new. It is simply not widespread or well-known. One example is Johnsonville Foods, a family-owned sausage company in Sheboygan, Wisconsin. CEO Ralph Stayer recalls that, in 1980, the company was in great shape, with profits above the industry average and a 20% annual growth rate.

However, one of Ralph's primary concerns was sustaining the company's competitive advantage. What worried him more than the competition itself was the gap between his own company's potential and its performance. Every day he came to work and saw people so bored by their jobs that they made dumb, thoughtless mistakes. As Ralph tells it, workers would show up in the morning, perform half-heartedly what they were told to do, and then go home. He wondered if the company could survive a serious competitive challenge with this low level of attentiveness and involvement. Without meaning to, he had developed a management style that placed every problem squarely on his shoulders. When he realized that *he* was the problem, he also realized that he could be the solution.

How CEO Ralph Did It

After coming to his second insight, that nothing matters more than a goal, Ralph realized that the most important question any manager can ask is, "In the best of all possible worlds, what would I really want to happen?" He then clarified his vision for the company, calling it "Point B": where he wanted the company to be. Point A, where the company was at that time, was a position of financial strength but unmotivated employees.

Next, Ralph conducted an employee survey; it revealed that people saw nothing for themselves at Johnsonville. Ralph realized that he had focused entirely on the financial side of the business. While his aggressive behavior and authoritarian practices with centralized control had grown the business, he had also created a huge obstacle to change and improvement.

Stayer took action by fixing himself first; he stopped solving all the problems and making all the decisions. He then changed the systems and structures that his autocratic management style had put in place. Next, he gave ownership of Johnsonville's problems to its employees, and allowed them to take responsibility for themselves and the business. Some of the changes included inviting sausage-making line workers to taste the product for themselves and to take ownership of the quality control system. When workers complained about the competence of fellow workers, Stayer invited them to take on the selection and training of new workers, so they gradually assumed the traditional personnel functions.

Best Place to Work to Become Great!

Employees now are self-starters, problem solvers, independent thinkers, and risk takers. One of Ralph's rewards is that Johnsonville can practically run without him. Today, Ralph has the following statement posted on the company website: "My first task is to be a developer of people—our organization's Members. It's a job that means I serve as a coach, supporter, and resource for making Members' lives fulfilling, challenging, and rewarding." - Ralph C. Stayer

Visitors to their website (www.johnsonville.com) are also invited to "check out our brochure and you will see why we consider Johnsonville the Best Place to Work for Members who want to become GREAT!"

Benefits of a Responsibility-Based Workplace

Imagine a work environment where all employees are fully engaged in their work and do whatever it takes to fulfill their responsibilities each day. You have hired good people, potential Top Talent, who are intrinsically motivated—the only sustainable motivation—by the work they do, and who are willing to hold themselves personally accountable.

From the Worker's Perspective

In a responsibility-based culture, everyone feels connected to the purpose and vision of the organization. They understand the importance of their jobs and have a sense of pride in what they do. They focus on the *purpose* of their activities, which causes workers to see those activities as making sense and having meaning. Workers receive an immediate, intrinsic reward that comes from the satisfaction of doing something significant. Making a contribution to the success of the enterprise provides a level of gratification and fulfillment that far outweighs extrinsic rewards.

From the Supervisors' and Managers' Perspective

Traditionally, managers simply want employees to do what they want them to do: Stick to the rules, follow procedures, and produce. This management style is based on the attitude that work is work, and if you are good, you will be paid more, get promoted, or receive some future reward.

The most immediate benefit for the managers and supervisors in a responsibility-based workplace is relief from the laborious task of monitoring workers, checking up on them, and attempting to motivate or influence their daily actions. Additionally, managers and supervisors have lower stress. They will experience improved job satisfaction by using their time and energy more productively in ways other than supervising, managing, and checking the output of workers.

High Payoff Activities

Using management time for high payoff activities is important for a number of reasons. Ask yourself, "What could managers and supervisors be doing if they had more time; what high payoff activities would be a better use of their time?" Assuming they're intrinsically motivated, managers and supervisors get to pursue what interests them most, thus increasing their level of personal fulfillment.

For example, suppose managers could use their time for planning, preventing problems, training and coaching their team and learning to master essential leadership skills. In a control-based workplace, there is limited time available for creativity, whereas in a trust-based environment supervisors simply become more visible and accessible to play the role of coach and mentor.

Consider creativity and innovation. Where does it come from? It will happen only if you make the time and space for it. Running around out of breath, adrenalized, and feeling under-the-gun will not produce many creative ideas.

Requirements for Accountability to Occur

The requirements for an accountability-based workplace include a leader with a compelling vision who will provide the resources and take the role of mentor/coach. With the accountability approach, managers trust people to own their jobs, to own the processes and systems, and to be accountable for their decisions and results. Visionary leaders believe in openness and flexibility and are willing to trust people to achieve the vision. They share their power and allow others to assume responsibility, a much more powerful approach than the traditional, autocratic take-charge approach. After all, people bestow true leadership on those they choose to follow.

This leadership approach attracts and retains Top Talent who want to show initiative and be open, creative, proactive, and responsible. An intention to turn good people into Top Talent acknowledges the need for a different style and a trust-based strategy. Making that shift can be a challenge for the highly directive manager who tends to use very authoritarian, control-based methods of supervision.

Readiness for a Responsibility-Based Culture

Here are ten critical questions that the senior leadership team must answer, understanding the commitment required. How these questions are answered will indicate if now is the right time to embark on the journey to transform your organization into a responsibility-based workplace.

1. Is a responsibility-based culture a high enough priority to ensure the necessary time and resources will be made available?

2. Will the organization be free from layoffs or merger within the near future? If not, transitioning to a responsibility-based culture may need to be delayed.

3. Will the senior executive (project sponsor) be around three to four years, long enough to see the transformation through?

4. Is the leadership of the organization committed to operating by the organization's values at all times?

5. Are the senior leaders of the organization prepared to deal appropriately with employees who are not willing to operate by the organization's values and the values that build trust?

6. Is the leadership of the organization committed to partnering with employees?

7. Does the nature of the work and the work schedule allow employees time to think, meet, and discuss ideas for improving performance?

8. Are employees technically competent in their work?

9. Is the leadership of the organization prepared to share power and control and abide by their decision to sponsor the transformation process?

10. Once committed to empowering employees, are the organization's leaders willing to stay with that decision?

(These questions were adapted from the work of Darcy Hitchcock in *Why Teams Can Fail and What to Do About It*, and Arlen Leholm and Ray Vlasin's *Increasing the Odds for High Performance Teams - Lessons Learned*.)

Steps to Creating a Responsibility-Based Workplace

When all the members of the senior team can affirmatively answer the ten readiness questions, I recommend an alignment process. The team must agree on the effect their decisions and behavior have on the organization's culture and the people skills they need to develop in order to create a culture that is based on trust and responsibility. They must also agree on the need to develop the people skills required to create a culture based on trust and responsibility. The senior team must further recognize how their team functions and the impact each team member's behavioral style has on the trust level within the team.

The alignment process should also address the seven critical steps for creating a responsibility-based workplace:

1. Ensure that all members of the senior team support the transformation process.

2. Get all senior team members "on the bus" and develop a plan to build a responsibility-based culture.

3. Benchmark the organization's culture and employee alignment, its vital signs. (This step is covered in detail in the next key.)

4. Get commitment from all managers and supervisors to support the transformation process, build trust, and create an environment where people become self-directed.

5. Create a values-based culture where employees operate by the organization's values and values that influence trust-building behaviors.

6. Provide all employees the opportunity to learn how to operate in a cross-functional task team.

7. Utilize cross-functional task teams to redesign processes, systems, and structures.

Each of these seven steps is covered in detail in Keys 2, 3 and 4. The process begins by having the members of the senior team complete the Team Alignment Questionnaire™ (TAQ). The TAQ measures the degree of alignment with purpose, vision, values, goals, procedures and roles and the trust levels among the members of the team. I will have more to say about team development in the coming pages.

Unless the senior team is prepared to take this approach, it may be more appropriate to begin with Key Five – Continuous Learning: Mastering the Essential Skills and Key Six – Coach-Based Management: Maximizing Worker and Manager Contribution. In these pages you will learn how to

- Improve your personal performance and results

- Manage both human and physical capital effectively

- Develop a flexible, participatory, open, and inclusive management style to foster engagement

- Ensure an empowering work environment that is cooperative, non-threatening, and supportive.

Now for a quick review of this section's Key Points, some questions to ponder, and a few assignments.

Key Points

➤   Workers must buy in to the results they are expected to accomplish and the methods they will use.

➤   The benefits for managers and supervisors of making the shift to an accountability-based organization include personal relief, reduced stress, and freedom to accomplish the high payoff activities that maximize their results.

➤   The ten misguided, control-based ideas that many organizations have implemented in an attempt to get workers to be accountable actually interfere with accountability.

➤   Accountability-based or values-based management *works*. Ralph Stayer is one example of a CEO who realized he needed to stop making all the decisions and let his workers lead.

➤   The senior team must consider ten critical questions to fully understand their commitment and what they need to do to make it work.

➤   Transforming an organization's culture requires the allocation of significant time and resources.

➤   Seven steps allow the transformation of your organization into a responsibility-based culture, beginning with getting alignment from top management to frontline supervisors. Ultimately, the process includes planning that involves all employees.

➤   Senior team alignment involves benchmarking the team's trust levels and the alignment with the six strategic elements mentioned above. This is followed by getting all senior team members "on the bus" and committed to developing a plan to build a responsibility-based culture.

➤   To ensure success in transforming your organization's
      culture, start by determining the level of readiness
      among the senior team.

Questions to Ponder

1. What would life be like for you if you had a responsibility-based
    workplace?

2. How many of the ten misguided ideas have you implemented? How
    can they be eliminated?

3. What are managers unable to get to because they're too busy con-
    trolling and supervising?

4. What high payoff activities are not being accomplished because of
    attention to lower payoff activities that accountable workers could
    perform?

5. How could managers begin to off-load some of their busy-ness
    by giving up control and creating an environment that empowers
    workers to become more personally accountable?

6. How could everyone become clearer about job accountabilities and
    specifically about what people are supposed to accomplish?

7. How do you describe your leadership style and its influence on employees' willingness to be accountable?

8. How do you think your management team will respond to the ten readiness questions?

TABS Action Plan

T. What was the main **thing** you got from this key?

A. What **action** are you willing to take?

B. What **benefit** do you expect to get from it?

S. What is the **single step** you will take to **get started** within 48 hours?

Assignments

→ Review with your management team the ten critical questions that indicate whether to begin the transformation process now. If the time is right, review the seven steps of the transformation process. Otherwise, discuss the importance of embarking on a leadership skill development process.

→ Measure the degree of alignment with purpose, vision, values, goals, procedures, and roles and the trust levels among the members of the team.

Next we will explore Key Two – Organizational Vitality: Attracting and Energizing Top Talent which includes benchmarking the organization's culture and assessing its vital signs in detail. If you're in a high state of readiness, this is the ideal place to begin the transformation journey.

Let's press on and examine the concept of organizational vitality!

KEY  TWO

ORGANIZATIONAL VITALITY:

ATTRACTING AND ENERGIZING TOP TALENT

"Companies should stop asking, 'What works at GE and Microsoft?' and start asking, 'What works here?'"
- **Haig Nalbantian, author of *Play to Your Strengths: Managing Your Internal Labor Markets for Lasting Competitive Advantage***

ORGANIZATIONAL VITALITY

T urning good people into Top Talent is intimately linked to organizational vitality. The more vitality an organization has, the more attractive it is to employees, customers, investors, suppliers, and other stakeholders.

Organizational Vitality

The term organizational vitality conveys the general state of health of an organization. The very word *vitality* brings to mind a picture of well-being, productivity, and progress. To achieve a compelling vision, organizations must be capable of continuous renewal and transformation while remaining steadfastly focused on the mission and purpose. In a "vital" organization, the strategic elements are effectively communicated to assure that everyone is in alignment.

Communication Effectiveness

An increase in market value as great as 30% can arise from significant improvements in communication effectiveness, according to numerous studies. Employee communication is no longer a "soft" function but rather a *business* function that drives performance and contributes to a company's financial success. Benchmarking the levels of clarity and approval of the organization's strategic elements establishes a point of reference, or baseline of communication effectiveness. The senior team has a major responsibility to continuously measure and attend to all elements that affect organizational vitality.

Benchmarking the Vital Signs

For our purposes, benchmarking is a *continuous, systematic process to gauge organizational improvement*. Haig Nalbantian, author of *Play to Your Strengths: Managing Your Internal Labor Markets for Lasting Competitive Advantage* and a principal of Mercer Human Resource Consulting, says, "We don't think enough organizations get to the point of evaluating, 'Where does the real value come from in our workforce?'"

Nalbantian argues for restacking the labor side of economic equations using human capital management that values skill and experience rather than simply tallying up the costs of hiring, training, and benefits. At the same time, he has little use for benchmarking against other companies, expending time and money to measure oneself against others. While a competitive view can help, the Mercer team suggests companies should stop asking, "What works at GE and Microsoft?" and start asking, "What works here?" I recommend exactly the same approach to clients by benchmarking and assessing their organization's vital signs.

As emphasized in the previous key, the CEO and all members of the senior team must be committed to supporting and being involved in the process of turning good people into Top Talent. This includes serious consideration of the ten questions in Key One that gauge whether the organization is ready to begin the transformation process. Additionally, the senior team must benchmark *themselves* to determine the level of alignment of the senior team. From there, they can proceed to benchmark the organization.

Let's begin by asking, what does a vital organization look like and what are the critical areas to measure?

The Four Critical Vital Signs

1. Alignment

When employees feel connected to the purpose and vision of the organization, they will have a clearer understanding of how important the products and services they provide are to customers and the community. They will also see the connection between what they do and how it relates to fulfilling the organization's purpose. As a result, aligned employees see their work as meaningful. They look forward to coming to work and have a sense of pride in their organization and in what they do.

For maximum employee commitment and involvement, everyone must fully align on six strategic elements:

1. **Purpose:** The reason your organization was created, why it exists, beyond making a profit

2. **Values:** How your organization operates and your commitment to standards

3. **Vision:** An expression of what the organization can become in the future

4. **Goals:** Short-term accomplishments in order to achieve your vision

5. **Procedures:** The specific steps required to achieve your goals

6. **Roles:** Specifically who is responsible for completing various steps toward your goals

> *To what degree are your employees aligned with your organization's purpose, values, goals, and procedures?*

2. Trust Levels

Most leaders believe they are trustworthy, but many behave in ways that diminish employees' and customers' trust for them and their company. Being trustworthy does not guarantee that you are *building trust*!

Trustworthiness involves the qualities of honesty, integrity, and truth-telling, while developing trust means instilling confidence in your dependability and believability. What is the trust level throughout your organization?

Benefits of High Trust Levels

Top Talent expects high levels of trust within the organization. When the organization consistently practices trust, the organization becomes a place where people eagerly come to work, turnover decreases, productivity and profitability increase, and customer satisfaction improves.

In a recent study of a national hotel chain, when employees believe strongly in their managers, their hotels are substantially more profitable than those where trust is average or low. So strong is the link that a one-eighth-point increase in trust on a five-point scale could be expected to increase the hotel's profitability by 2.5% of revenues. In this study, 2.5% of revenues translated into a profit increase of more than $250,000 per year per hotel.

Management Behavior and the Bottom Line

Intentions do not build trust! To maximize business results, leaders must develop and consistently practice the skills required to create an environment based on trust.

Research consistently shows a direct relationship between management behavior and culture. Managers throughout the organization must recognize that the way they behave and treat employees establishes the organization's climate. That climate then becomes the culture, which in turn directly influences bottom line, measurable results. If you hire talented people, is there any reason not to trust them?

The late W. Edwards Deming frequently asked management groups, "How many of you would say that you have dead wood in your organization?" Nearly everyone would raise their hands, and then Deming would ask, "Well, did you hire them that way? Or did you just kill them off?"

3. Values That Build Trust

Ultimately, our values or belief system determines whether or not we will take a certain action. Research conducted by Integro Leadership Institute, with which I am affiliated, has identified the following eight values as influencing trust-building behaviors:

1. **Straightforwardness**—Being clear about what is expected of employees

2. **Honesty**—Having high standards of honesty in everything they do

3. **Receptivity**—Giving new ideas and methods a fair hearing

4. **Disclosure**—Communicating openly one's own ideas and opinions

5. **Respect**—Valuing others for who they are

6. **Recognition**—Getting the recognition they deserve

7. **Seeking Excellence**—Striving to be the best in everything

8. **Keeping Commitments**—Following through on their promises

When people agree to operate by these values, trust-building behaviors are more likely to occur, provided they have developed trust-building skills.

4. Employee Engagement

A recent Gallup Survey of 19,000 U.S. workers found that 71% of employees are either unengaged (just putting in their time) or are *actively disengaged*. The actively disengaged are not only unproductive and unhappy, they also spread their discontent. These employees are also known as the CAVE Dwellers: They are Consistently Against Virtually Everything! This leaves only 29% of the workforce engaged, loyal, and productive. Thus, the businesses surveyed operate at less than one-third of their capacity.

Cost of Worker Disengagement

Let's calculate the cost for a 100-person organization with a payroll of $5 million (average pay and benefits of $50,000 per year). If the engaged employees are giving 100% of their capability, but 70% of employees are unengaged or actively disengaged, operating at 50% of their capability, the cost to the organization is 35% of payroll, or $1,750,000.

What is their level of worker engagement in *your* organization?

In the coming pages, I will cover strategies to increase the level of worker engagement, a key to turning good people into Top Talent.

Measuring the Vital Signs

Assess these four vital signs initially as a benchmark and then again at predetermined intervals to measure improvement. In working with organizations to transform the culture, I use a tool developed by Integro Learning Company called the Strategic Alignment Survey™ (SAS) The SAS benchmarks the organization's vital signs and provides the basis for effectively targeting strengths and areas that need improvement. The SAS provides an objective measure of the levels of trust and strategic alignment within the organization. The survey also identifies existing organizational challenges and uncovers issues that need to be addressed to create a responsibility-based culture.

The SAS report, which can be provided by division, business unit, location, or work teams within the organization, reveals the following essential information about your organization.

Section One — Kinds of People

Based on the personal responsibility model developed by Dr. Ralph Colby, cofounder of Integro Learning Company, this section of the SAS measures employees' perceptions of the behavior of their co-workers. The personal responsibility model divides the workforce into three kinds of people: self-directed, compliant, and rebellious. It offers a snapshot of how the employees behave at a given time and is not necessarily a portrait of the group.

Questions to Consider

1. In what ways does your organization's present leadership approach influence employees' efforts to become self-directed?

2. What kind of culture would attract and retain self-directed people, and guide those rebellious and compliant employees to behave in a self-directed way?

Section Two — The Trust Level Report

The team trust level report measures the degree to which each employee perceives the following four Elements of Trust™ in their work group:

1. **Congruence**: The degree to which employees are willing to practice what they preach, and alignment of intentions and actions

2. **Openness**: The degree to which employees openly share information and opinions, and are comfortable receiving feedback, discussing feelings, and revealing relevant information to one another

3. **Acceptance**: The degree to which employees feel listened to, accepted for who they are, safe to express conflicting views, and able to encourage and support each other

4. **Reliability**: The degree to which employees can rely on each other to get the job done, do what they say they will do, take ownership of their jobs, and consistently operate with high standards of quality.

Of the four elements, acceptance is often the most underrated, and yet it is critical in order to create the climate for the other three elements to increase.

When team members feel valued and respected, they feel more comfortable being open and honest with one another.

Questions to Consider

1. Which of the Elements of Trust™ do you think is strongest for you, your team, and the organization? Which is the weakest?

2. What are the factors that contribute to your strengths? Which factors need improvement?

3. What barriers need to be removed to increase the trust level?

Section Three — Values That Build Trust

The following eight values must be present to *drive* trust-building behaviors:

1. Straightforwardness
2. Honesty
3. Receptivity
4. Disclosure
5. Respect
6. Recognition
7. Seeking Excellence
8. Keeping Commitments

Values Gap

Measuring the gap between how important these values are and the degree to which they are practiced provides an indication of the level of organizational credibility. Minimizing the gaps between the personal values people *expect* and what they *experience* enhances belief in the organization and can have a significant impact on commitment.

The Strategic Alignment Survey questionnaire asks respondents two questions about each of the eight values that build trust:

1. How important is this value to you personally?

2. How well does your organization operate by this value?

The size of the gap between the personal importance of the value to the respondents and their estimation of the organization's performance in terms of the value is then displayed on a bar chart. The following is an example of the results of one of the values measured.

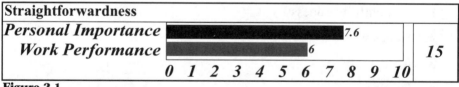

Straightforwardness		
Personal Importance	7.6	
Work Performance	6	**15**
0 1 2 3 4 5 6 7 8 9 10		

Figure 2.1

The amount of the gap can have a significant impact on employee engagement and commitment. If employees indicate that these values are "important" to "very important" to them and then rate the "organization's performance" significantly lower, they are saying, "This is important to me, but my organization doesn't operate this way."

Questions to Consider

1. Which of the eight values do you believe are most important to the people in your organization?

2. How much of a gap do you think exists between these values' perceived importance and actual practice in your organization?

3. What needs to change for everyone to operate by these values?

Section Four - Group Alignment Report

The group alignment report illustrates the degree of clarity and personal approval for each of the six strategic elements: purpose, values, vision, goals, procedures and roles (Figure 2.2). The personal approval level of each respondent is illustrated by the expression on the face.

A smiling face 😊 = approval.

A frowning face ☹ = disapproval.

The neutral face 😐 is somewhere in between, neither approving nor disapproving.

A number next to a face indicates how many respondents are in that category.

Respondents indicate the degree of clarity they believe exists among the members of the group for each of the six elements. That score is represented by the position of the faces on the horizontal scale.

The percentages for team clarity and team approval are relative to 100%.

Scores will assist you in determining an action plan to address each category. For example, the lowest score represents the greatest opportunity for improvement.

Figure 2.2 Group Alignment Report

	Very Unclear	Moderately Unclear		Moderately Clear		Very Clear	Team Clarity	Team Approval
Purpose			☺1	☺4 ☹1	☺5	☺4	81.0%	83.3%
Values	☺1	☺1	☺1	☺2 ☺1	☺6	☺3	73.35%	88.9%
Vision		☺1 ☹2	☺2 ☺3	☺1 ☺1	☺5		60.0%	73.3%
Goals	☹1		☺3 ☺1 ☹1	☺2	☺5	☺2	67.8%	77.8%
Procedures	☹1	☺2	☺1 ☺1 ☹1	☺1 ☺2	☺4 ☺2		62.2%	72.2%
Roles	☹1		☺1	☺3 ☺1	☺1 ☺2	☺5 ☹1	78.9%	71.1%

Position= Clarity, Countenance =Approval

Overall Group Alignment: Clarity 70.5%, Approval: 77.8

Application of the SAS Report

When the Strategic Alignment Survey is complete, the SAS Report can focus attention on those strategic elements or categories measured that need the most attention to increase clarity and/or approval. Following a debriefing with the senior executive or project sponsor, the entire senior management team will then participate in a half-day feedback session to discuss the following questions:

1. With which of the six strategic elements measured by the SAS is the group _most_ in alignment?

2. With which of six strategic elements is the group _least_ in alignment?

3. What are the implications of the survey's findings?

4. Which of the six strategic elements received the least approval? Which received the most?

One of the objectives of the feedback session is to gain senior management agreement on the importance of developing trust-building skills and to be willing to model trust-building behaviors. When trust-building is a priority, your organization becomes one in which information is exchanged freely as needed, feelings and opinions are openly discussed, and people have no hidden agendas. Expectations will be clear, disagreements openly discussed and resolved, and individual performance discussed and agreed on without having to rely on a formal process. With high levels of trust-building skills, differences among individuals are valued, and employees feel respected for their contributions, and have input into ways the organization can be more successful. Finally, people keep their commitments, strive for excellence in everything they do, and can count on each other for support.

These signs of well-being are direct indicators of how well the talent within your organization is performing.

Other Measures of Vitality: In-Process vs. End-Process Measurements

The vital signs that have been covered up to now are *in-process measurements*, which measure what is happening *while it is happening*, such as trust levels within a team or the level of agreement on the elements of a strategy. In the same way a thermostat tells you the current temperature so you can take action to adjust it, in-process measurement of your organization's vital signs provides the basis for adjustments.

End-process measurements show *what has happened in the past*, over which you no longer have direct control. These measures are not used to determine organizational vitality and will obviously have no effect on those customers or employees who have already left your company. However, they can help you to make adjustments that may have an impact in the future. End-process measurements establish a trend of progress toward or away from an objective. Those which measure past performance are most valuable as a score card against which a future score can be compared.

Let's consider three end-process measurements and their importance as an indicator of symptoms that may require closer examination. These measures themselves do not generally provide any indication of *causes* but are rather an indication of *effect*.

1. Employee Satisfaction and Retention

- What measures are you using to determine work expectations and the degree they are met?

- What are the reasons people leave your organization?

- How do employee turnover levels at your company compare to the standards for your industry?

- What insights can you gain from a Strategic Alignment Survey that may be a warning that something needs attention?

2. Customer Satisfaction

Even though customer satisfaction is not directly a vital sign, measuring it provides a benchmark of your talent's output or effectiveness, offering evidence of the progress your organization is making toward maximizing your competitive advantage.

Many organizations routinely survey customers to determine the quality of the experience. Have you ever filled out a comment card in a hotel? As a customer, I frequently receive requests from companies to go online and provide feedback. One such survey from a hotel resulted in the replacement of an article I had left behind after checking out. The use of "mystery shoppers" is becoming a popular process used by many retail organizations to obtain current, real-time "customer" feedback.

Did you know?

- Recent studies estimate that it costs five to seven times as much to acquire a new customer as it does to keep one you already have.

- You have some control over 97% of the reasons customers stop doing business with you and direct control over 68%.

- *The Harvard Business Review* article, "Zero Defections: Quality Comes to Service," reports that as a customer's relationship with a company lengthens, profits can rise by almost 100% by retaining 5% more customers.

Top Talent tend to be more effective and treat customers better, which allows you to maximize your competitive advantage; it is your Top Talent who will exceed your customers' expectations by delivering unanticipated value.

3. Sales and Marketing Effectiveness

What is the primary function of your sales force, its primary accountability? Some companies charge their sales force with a single objective: to increase revenue. This often leaves the individual sales person with the option to use whatever methods will get immediate sales results, regardless of customer satisfaction levels. To maximize your competitive advantage, the sales force of today must become Top Talent who see their role as adding value for the customer. Rather than focusing on just making sales, a superior performing sales force must assure that customers receive value.

The most effective sales force will focus on progressive and strategic level clients who want added value, not just expected value. A strategic-level client is more inclined toward a collaborative relationship in which buyer and sales person are partners in providing solutions rather than just placing and taking orders. The progressive buyer moves along the pathway from a commodity buy to a strategic buy and may need some education and cultivation. For example, I consider myself to be a strategic buyer, particularly when it comes to professional services. I always look for a source that will provide a service that creates value beyond the expected level.

Recently, while searching for a publicist, I found a wide range of responsiveness to my e-mail and website inquiries. Within 24 hours, one firm had responded and suggested we set a phone appointment and have a conversation. During that conversation, I not only felt understood and valued, I also received several useful ideas even before I expressed any intention of doing business with them.

What impact would it make on your business if all of your customers were strategic or progressive buyers?

Both In-processs and End-process measures are direct indicators of how well the talent within your organization is performing. However, only In-process measures provide real-time feedback and the basis for corrective action. Benchmarking alignment, trust levels, values that build trust, and employee engagement, along with other critical measures, such as employee retention and customer satisfaction levels, will provide you with a clear picture of organizational strengths and show you the challenges you may encounter on your way to a successful transformation process.

Senior Leadership Coaching

To ensure a successful transformation process, two critical roles must be fulfilled:

1. *The sponsor*—who is usually the CEO or the senior leader— allocates the resources and makes the process a top priority.

2. *The co-agents* of the process—usually the senior management team—see that the appropriate steps are taken at the right time. They become the primary implementers of the tactical action steps throughout the journey.

The senior leader must effectively fill both of these roles with the commitment of the senior management team. The senior leader needs to be both the sponsor *and* a co-agent. In other words, an organizational transformation process requires continuous senior level involvement to achieve positive long-term results.

Additionally, targets of the transformation will feel the impact of required changes and be personally transformed by the process. An example might be a middle manager who must shift to a more participatory behavioral style and become a coach-based manager rather than a traditional autocrat who plays the role of boss. High levels of willingness are required to make these changes in style and behavior. These changes must occur first with the sponsors and agents of the process.

Filling these roles and being a willing target of the personal transformations that may be required are not small tasks and generally require extraordinary skill and personal commitment. The best way to develop these skills is with the support of a masterful coach-based consultant. Coach-based consultants are rare, so it is unlikely your organization has one internally.

A masterful coach-based consultant effectively combines the two disciplines of coaching and consulting toward a common outcome: achieving organizational results while addressing the skills and needs of the individual being coached. This dual role is required to gather and interpret the results of feedback from surveys, assessments, and other instruments and to help the client to interpret the data, and then create an appropriate plan of action to improve or enhance organizational and personal effectiveness. This balance is essential when working with senior leaders who are sponsors and co-agents of a transformational process.

A masterful coach-based consultant will challenge your intentions so that you can deliver meaningful results; he or she will also provide a sounding board to support your progress toward becoming more accountable for decisions and choices.

Here are the steps I take when guiding my coach clients:

1. Identify the crucial needs of the situation and environment.

2. Measure the individual's ability to meet those needs.

3. Interview others to help pinpoint specific strengths and weaknesses in the individual being coached.

4. Create relevance between what talents the person has or does not have, and the impact that has on performance.

5. Help to set solid, achievable, and measurable goals that support the situation.

6. Provide accountability to ensure progress and compliance.

7. Bring new expertise and knowledge to help expand understanding and teach new techniques to achieve success.

8. Provide a stable, standardized system wherein all of this can take place effectively.

9. Use personal influence to calm, motivate, reassure, and inspire the individual.

10. Act as confidante and sounding board in making decisions.

Ultimately, all executives, managers, and leaders within the organization must adopt a coach-based management approach, the subject of Key Six. Members of the senior leadership team set the example of what an effective leader does by modeling new behavior and demonstrating mastery of the essential leadership skills such as self-management, setting realistic expectations, and evaluating and helping others to develop.

A masterful coach-based consultant can provide resources and information, a fresh perspective, feedback, observations and insights to improve the leadership skills of the highly motivated, coachable executive. Ideally, the consultant will also deliver unanticipated value by going far beyond expected outcomes and even beyond value added.

Most of my colleagues and I look for opportunities to provide services that are not a part of the original agreement in order to achieve the intended result. For example, in many cases an additional day of facilitation is required to complete an action planning session, or another phone coaching session is required to keep the project on track. I provide these value-added services since I focus on the intended outcome rather than on the time I put into the project.

In what ways do *you* provide something extra and unexpected to your customer in order to add value to the relationship and move it beyond a simple transaction?

Visionary leaders can expect the ideal relationship with a masterful coach-based consultant to be a strategic partnership that is personally transforming, not merely a find-and-fix transaction.

In Key Three, we will examine a critical key that must be in place for turning good people into Top Talent: "Shared Values: Assuring Credibility that Builds Trust."

Key Points

➤ The term *organizational vitality* conveys the general state of health of an organization. There are four critical vital signs:

1. Alignment—establishing a baseline of communication effectiveness; clarity of the organization's six strategic elements: purpose, values, vision, goals, procedures and roles

2. The level of trust within the group, team or organizational unit as indicated by congruence, openness, acceptance, and reliability

3. Values that build trust indicate the degree to which people will engage in trust-building behaviors

4. Engagement Levels of Workers

➤ The Strategic Alignment Survey™ (SAS) is an effective process for benchmarking the critical vital signs. When repeated at predetermined intervals, the SAS process provides concrete evidence of improvements.

➤ In-process measures show current conditions as they are happening.

➤ Employee retention and satisfaction, customer service, and sales and marketing effectiveness are examples of end-process measures.

➤ Leadership must agree to sponsor the transformation process, implement the steps and model appropriate leadership behavior.

➤ A masterful coach-based consultant provides the visionary leader with the support and guidance to ensure a successful journey with positive outcomes.

Questions to Ponder

1. How clear are your managers about the distinction between trustworthiness and trust?

2. How important is it to have everyone within your organization aligned with your purpose, values, and vision?

3. How effective is the communication level in your organization regarding purpose, values, vision, goals, procedures and roles? How high is clarity and agreement?

4. What are the trust levels? How wide is the values gap?

5. What percentages of the people within your organization are self-directed, compliant, or rebellious?

6. How valuable could it be for you to get a measurement of your organization's vital signs?

TABS Action Plan

T . What was the main **thing** you got from this key?

A . What **action** are you willing to take?

B . What **benefit** do you expect to get from it?

S . What is the **single step** you will take to **get started** within 48 hours?

Assignments

- Determine your organization's vital signs and how you will measure them.

- Engage a masterful coach-based consultant to facilitate a top management discussion about what it really takes to establish a responsibility-based culture, the first key to turning good people into Top Talent.

KEY  THREE

SHARED VALUES:

ASSURING CREDIBILITY THAT BUILDS TRUST

"When aligned around shared values and united in a common purpose, ordinary people accomplish extraordinary results and give their organization a competitive edge.

- Ken Blanchard and Mike O'Connor,
co-authors of *Managing By Values*

SHARED VALUES

An established and reinforced set of positive operational and personal values is essential to attracting and fully utilizing Top Talent. Operational values are often referred to as "business values." Business values define how the organization and its people operate. You may even consider a set of business values as the organizational operating system (OS). Just as a computer needs an operating system to functional effectively, an organization must have an operating system as well. This OS becomes the principles and practices that everyone must utilize. Adopting and practicing a set of core business values is critical to attracting and retaining Top Talent and to maintaining positive relationship with customers, employees, and other stakeholders.

Much attention has been paid to American businesses that focus more on the bottom line—on producing revenues—than on how they operate. Business scandals involving Enron, WorldCom, Tyco, Adelphia, HealthSouth, Global Crossing, the New York Stock Exchange, and others have raised issues about corporate responsibility to the community and the workforce. Employees, like shareholders, lenders, and potential investors, expect more transparency today from the organizations in which they invest their talents. Organizations of all types risk long-term disaster unless they shift their focus to operating by a set of core values.

Even the military recently discovered the need to establish a set of core values to guide the behavior of combat troops in Iraq. Following allegations that Marines killed two dozen unarmed civilians in Haditha in November 2005, the military ordered the implementation of values or ethics training, including slide shows, for the 150,000 coalition troops in Iraq. The number two-ranking U.S. general in Iraq, Lt. Gen. Peter Chiarelli said, "As military professionals, it is important that we take time to reflect on the values that separate us from our enemies." The training will focus on values and ethics that everyone in uniform in Iraq needs to adhere to. Hopefully, this approach will go beyond what could appear to be a too-little-too-late, quick-fix approach to modifying core issues.

In the previous chapter, Organizational Vitality, I discussed the importance of benchmarking the vital signs. Alignment, the first vital sign mentioned, refers to the importance of clarity and agreement on purpose, vision, and values. Measure the degree to which everyone, beginning with the senior team, commit to operating standards.

In my consulting work, I frequently hear managers complain about people not following the procedures that were put in place to meet standards of customers' and other stakeholders' satisfaction. Upon closer examination, I find that these employees are rarely given reasons for the procedures, so they typically resist what seems to them to be details that waste time and slow production. To more easily achieve buy-in, management must involve everyone in the process of establishing values-based guidelines and standards.

Management Commitment

Many question the integrity of management and leadership, and the level of trust in the workplace is at an all-time low. Even before the corporate scandals at the beginning of the 21st century, there was agreement among leaders within Corporate America that unless companies continually demonstrate their commitment to business values like honesty, integrity, fairness, and cooperation—not profits alone—they are in big trouble.

To establish credibility with their employees as well as their customer base, executives must lead by example and serve as role models for the organization's values. Leaders at all levels should model core values and actively identify new areas for their own personal growth.

Many executives are just now realizing the importance of an established and reinforced set of core values to positively influence how people operate. The new foundation for organizational effectiveness is purpose, vision, and values. With a commitment to shared values and common goals, everyone is inspired to be responsible and accountable for personal performance.

To what extent does everyone understand your organization's values and agree to operate by them?

The Impact of Shared Values

Walter Industries, headquartered in Tampa, Florida, was once described as "an ill-defined conglomerate." The original company, the Jim Walter Corporation, had been characterized as being an "if it ain't broke, don't fix it" kind of organization. In late 2000, the leadership of Walter Industries implemented a Commitment to Excellence process built on vision, values, strategy, and operating excellence. The team created the Walter Industries' jigsaw puzzle (Figure 3.1).

Figure 3.1

This was a dramatic change from the way the company had been operating. Management gave employees a chance to discuss these new sets of values and either buy in or not buy in to them. Meanwhile, contrary behaviors not consistent with the values and norms expected were deemed inappropriate, and then dealt with so that individuals either subscribed to the accepted behaviors or ultimately left the company.

To bring about a successful culture shift initiative, senior leadership began looking for ways to grow truly energized people. Since then, most employees have embraced the new culture. Internal surveys show the newly-involved workers are happier now than before the cultural shift.

In my experience of working with an organization that was going through a cultural transformation, managers commonly resist giving up control and authority. Autocratic, control-based behavior must shift to a more respectful, collaborative style that consistently allows workers to assume more responsibility than they were previously allowed.

Reinforcement and Recognition

The Walter Industries Commitment to Excellence Process and associated initiatives are not just programs of the month or catchy slogans. Previously, the company did not fully tap its internal knowledge and skill-set. Now, employees at all levels throughout the company are reinforced, rewarded, and recognized for their ability to work in groups, think creatively, and live the core values. The implementation of a system of rewards, recognition, and acknowledgment has been essential to assure success of the process.

Twice a year the company gives out a set of core value awards, choosing an individual or group that has embodied each core value. Each winner, chosen from nominations submitted by employees, receives 100 shares of Walter Industries stock. Since launching the program, Walter Industries has recognized and awarded stock to employees who demonstrate examples of operating by the Walter Industries core values: integrity, customer commitment, high performance culture, fleetness of foot, innovation (cutting approximately $50,000 in cost through new ways of scheduling), accountability, respect for others, and teamwork.

The Pay-Off

The transformation efforts are beginning to pay off. Because of the culture shift, many more people are engaged and more openly seek advice and counsel. They rapidly implement change and feel empowered to give the company the full use of their skills and capabilities. They are becoming Top Talent.

People Values

The results of a University of Chicago study based on 17 million surveys of workers in 40 countries around the world revealed what people wanted in their work environment in order to be productive and creative. These "Eight Shared Values of the Heroic Environment" are discussed in the book *Lasting Change: The Shared Values Process That Makes Companies Great* written by Rob Lebow and William Simon. Since the values of an organization determine how people behave every day, they can be easily observed and measured. By measuring how people deal with each other, it is possible to predict performance levels and commitments to service and quality standards. The degree to which people share these values determines the level of behavior-based trust present within an organization.

In working with organizations that want to improve performance over the past 30 years, I have discovered that a values conflict underlies most performance issues. As a result of a customer survey, one of my clients recently attempted to implement a change in the standard operations procedure to assure higher quality results and greater customer satisfaction. A small management committee was assigned to create a document that outlined the procedures that all staff were expected to follow. It should not come as a surprise to anyone that the resistance to these changes has resulted in their limited application.

What could have been done better or differently? First, any change, particularly those that involve a perceived threat or additional effort, must be preceded with significant levels of involvement throughout the organization. Further, all changes must support one or more of the organization's shared values. The values an organization puts forth must be regarded as essential to achieving the vision and purpose. Thus, it comes down to leadership at all levels who will not only model the value-based behavior, but will also continuously represent the organization's vision and purpose to all the people. This underscores the principle that values are "caught" and not "taught" which the U.S. military may discover in attempting to "teach" values to the troops in Iraq.

Values That Build Trust

Ultimately, our values or belief system determines what action we take. The following eight values, mentioned in Chapter Two, influence trust-building behaviors:

1. **Straightforwardness**—Being clear about what is expected of employees

2. **Honesty**—Having high standards of truthfulness in everything they do

3. **Receptivity**—Giving new ideas and methods a fair hearing

4. **Disclosure**—Openly communicating their own ideas and opinions

5. **Respect**—Being valued for who they are

6. **Recognition**—Getting the recognition they deserve

7. **Seeking Excellence**—Striving to be the best in everything

8. **Keeping Commitments**—Following through on their promises

Trust-building behaviors are more likely to occur when people operate by these values, provided they have developed trust-building skills.

Measuring the gap between how important these values are and the degree to which they are practiced provides an indication of the level of organizational credibility. Minimizing the gaps between these personal values people *expect* and what they *experience* enhances trust.

Transforming Your Organization's Culture

An organization cannot forcibly or hurriedly switch over to a program of managing by values. You may create the appearance that things are different on the outside, but real change happens *within* people, in the way they respond to situations. In my experience, and in those of my colleagues of the Integro Leadership Institute, it may take two or three years for an organizational culture change process to take hold and really start yielding consistent business returns.

Begin by measuring the levels of clarity and approval of vision and values, covered in Chapter Two (Benchmarking Vital Signs). Implementing a plan to increase clarity and approval, and closing the gap in trust-building behaviors is a step toward maximizing engagement, retention, and utilization of Top Talent. More will be said about this in the next chapter, beginning with senior management becoming an extraordinary team.

Creating a Values-Based Workplace

In Chapter One, I outlined the steps to create a responsibility-based workplace. Chapter Two covered benchmarking the vital signs. Based on the results of the Strategic Alignment Survey (SAS), you are now ready to embark on the process of creating greater alignment, beginning with the senior team. That is the subject of the next chapter, High Performing Teams. Toward the end of that process, it will be time to involve all levels of the organization in creating a values-based workplace.

Since this chapter is about shared values and their importance in turning good people into Top Talent, I will briefly describe that process now. The process begins by gaining agreement that the gaps between the level of personal preference for each of the values that build trust, and the degree to which people operate by those values, must become smaller. This step is part of the debrief of the SAS described in the last chapter.

Next, involve all employees in a series of highly participative workshops designed by Integro Leadership Institute which can be facilitated by the organization's in-house trainer following certification or a pilot project presented by an Integro Associate. In addition to a thorough discussion of the Elements of Trust™, participants explore each of the eight values that build trust. This series begins by posing the following questions:

Do your organization's core values pass the following test?

1. Are they relevant to everyone in the organization? Yes No

2. Are they something that we must do to succeed? Yes No

3. Is it within our control to ensure that this happens? Yes No

4. Are they inspirational? Yes No

Putting our values into action

- What are the benefits from living by our organization's values:
  - ○ To the organization?
  - ○ To my team?
  - ○ To me individually?

- Where are we currently doing a good job of living our organization's values?

- What are the barriers to us doing a better job of living our organization's values?

- What are some things we can do to better operate by our organization's values?

Here is an example of what is covered in one of the workshop sessions:

Explore Value 1: Respect
- Experience the feelings that arise when you are and are not shown respect.

- Identify things people do in the workplace that demonstrate respect or fail to show respect.

Guidelines for adhering to the value of respect
- Develop a specific set of behavioral guidelines to use to promote the consistent practice of respect in our workplace.

Explore Value 2: Recognition
- Experience the feelings that arise when you are and are not given recognition.

- Identify things people do in the workplace to show recognition or demonstrate a lack of recognition.

Guidelines for adhering to the value of recognition
- Determine the impact on our workplace of consistently practicing the values of recognition.

How respect and recognition help us live our business values
- Determine the impact on our workplace of consistently practicing the values of respect and recognition.

- Identify and explain how demonstrating respect and recognition will help the organization live its business values.

- Build a commitment to demonstrate respect, recognition and all of the organization's business values.

Transferring Learning into Action
- List the individual actions you will take in order to bring what you have learned in this meeting to your daily work.

Shared Values Summary

Fully engaged Top Talent results from individuals who operate within a trust-based environment and are willing to hold themselves accountable for practicing the organization's core people and business values. When everyone in the organization practices these behaviors consistently, they becomes highly credible, not only with employees, but to customers, vendors, and other stakeholders.

Key Points

➤ The new foundation for organizational effectiveness is purpose, vision, and values.

➤ A commitment to shared values and common goals is critical to inspiring everyone to be responsible and accountable for personal performance.

➤ The level of trust in the workplace is at an all-time low, so executives must lead by example and serve as role models for the organization's values.

➤ Walter Industries provides an example of an organizational transformation process based on vision and core values. The involvement of their people is key to the success of their culture shift initiative.

➤ An organization cannot be forcibly or hurriedly switched over to managing by values. The transformation process may take two or three years to take hold and really start yielding consistent business returns.

➤ By measuring how people deal with each other, it is possible to predict performance levels and commitments to service and quality standards.

➤ Core values are "caught" and not "taught."

➤ Creating a values-based workplace requires involvement from everyone in the organization including participation in a highly interactive workshop series.

➤ When behaviors based on core values are practiced consistently by everyone, the organization's credibility is enhanced with employees, customers, vendors, and other stakeholders.

Questions to Ponder

1. How important do you believe it is to operate by a set of core values in *your* company?

2. What process have you used to assure alignment of your organization's core values? How will you communicate this?

3. What methods are you and leaders at all levels using to reinforce your organization's values?

4. What are some of the benefits of strengthening your organization's foundation based on trust and shared values?

5. What will be the ultimate outcome of your organization making the shift to a values-based workplace?

TABS Action Plan

T. What was the main **thing** you got from this chapter?

A. What **action** are you willing to take?

B. What **benefit** do you expect to get from it?

S. What is the **single step** you will take to **get started** within 48 hours?

Assignments

- Identify your company's core values and determine how you will communicate them and reinforce them.

- If you already have established core values, revisit them in a way that garners a commitment to operate by them.

KEY  FOUR

HIGH PERFORMING TEAMS:
ACHIEVING EXTRAORDINARY RESULTS

"A team remains the most flexible and most powerful unit of performance, learning, and change in any organization."
 - Jon Katzenbach and Douglas Smith, *The Wisdom of Teams*

HIGH PERFORMING TEAMS

In Key One, I recommended an alignment process that begins with the senior team completing the Team Alignment Questionnaire (TAQ). The TAQ measures the degree of clarity and approval within the team on purpose, vision, values, goals, procedures and roles and the level of trust. In this key on high performing teams, I will discuss the application of the results of the TAQ in the development of the senior team.

Senior Team Development

Senior Team Development begins with a senior team planning process focused on increasing clarity and approval on purpose, vision, values, and goals. By the time the senior team has completed the alignment process, the team will have raised trust levels within the team, increased alignment within the team on the purpose, vision, values, and goals. The next stage includes a process for developing an action plan to establish a responsibility-based culture and a values-based workplace built on the results of benchmarking the organization's vital signs as described in the last key.

When the senior team is aligned and models trust-building behaviors it sets an example for the rest of the organization. Creating high performing teams at all levels is the ultimate approach to achieving the innovative breakthroughs that provide customers the value-added responsiveness they want.

In their book, *The Wisdom of Teams*, Jon Katzenbach and Douglas Smith say, "We believe that teams—real teams, not just groups that management calls "teams"—should be the basic unit of performance for most organizations, regardless of size."

What is a Team?

A real team is a small number of people with complementary skills who are committed to a common purpose, performance goals, and approach for which they hold themselves mutually accountable. Katzenbach and Smith define a *high-performance team* as a group that meets all the conditions of a real team and also has members who are deeply committed to one another's personal growth and success. This is distinct from groups who may simply call themselves a team, such as

- **Working groups**—no significant incremental performance need or opportunity that requires it to become a team

- **Pseudo-teams**—could have a significant, incremental performance need or opportunity but have not focused on collective performance and are not trying to achieve it

- **Potential teams**—have a significant incremental performance need and are trying to improve their performance.

Groups That Benefit From Team Development

<u>Project Teams</u>—Project teams often get stuck before they get started while members get to know each other, sort out ego conflicts, and develop a process for working together.

<u>Quality or Continuous Improvement Teams</u>—Quality teams often lack the balance needed to be truly innovative. Some have great ideas, but they lack the analytical and implementation skills necessary for turning ideas into reality.

Many work teams do not function as teams but as a group of people who work together every day, without capitalizing on the benefits of effective teamwork. By taking time out to clarify purpose, vision, values and goals, these teams can significantly improve their output. Individual team members also gain more satisfaction from their work.

<u>Senior Management Teams</u>—Many senior management teams battle with conflicting priorities, politics, a lack of clarity and agreement on the organization's vision, and goals. Senior management teams need a structure to align team members and remove the politics to achieve optimal results. The team leading your organization—above all others—must work together cohesively and innovatively to provide the leadership your organization needs to succeed.

Challenges of the Senior Team

In cultures that reward individual performance, getting people who spend most of their time working alone to become fully participating members of high-performing teams can be challenging, particularly among senior leadership. Most members of the senior team are accountable for a department, function, or business unit within the organization, and their individual accountability is extremely important. Jon Katzenbach adds his caution to the subject in his book *Teams at the Top*, "...we all know that these so-called top teams seldom function as real teams because of the pressures of other priorities, as well as their strong desire to preserve individual accountability, if not ego."

To become a highly effective member of the senior team requires team members to understand that these team responsibilities will require different behaviors. They may need to learn new skills so that strong individual contributors can function together effectively within the senior team.

A systematic team development process beginning with the executive team is the most effective approach to creating and executing a strategy that will maximize business results. It typically will yield eight benefits:

1. Greater appreciation for team strengths

2. Stronger team spirit and cohesion

3. More effectively dealing with change

4. Measurable increase in trust level

5. Open, straightforward communication

6. Increased ability to overcome roadblocks to goals

7. Greater team responsibility for performance

8. Increased contribution from all team members

Assuring Success

The most important ingredients for team success are a clear and compelling performance challenge along with the commitment to work together effectively to address it. Unless the performance challenge is meaningful, individuals may lack the motivation needed to develop effective team member skills. It may require further effort to balance team and individual accountabilities to achieve the results expected of a high performing team. When the team is given an objective or challenge, such as to produce a product superior to the competition's in record time, members become stimulated and energized to work together to achieve it.

President Kennedy's vision of putting a man on the moon provided that kind of challenge. Not many companies will have that kind of vision, but exceptional ones do: Think of those who rallied to build the Panama Canal, invent the first computer or a better computer or a faster microprocessor.

What compelling challenges exist for *your* company that only a talented team could achieve?

In addition to a compelling performance challenge, the degree to which the following conditions are present can help determine if team development is a worthwhile investment.

- Current level of interaction among team members is inadequate for high performance; however, team members understand that significant interaction is expected of them.

- All team members are willing to commit their full abilities to achieving maximum results.

- Team members share the belief that working together is better than working in isolation.

- Team members understand that they must coordinate their efforts for effective planning and decision-making.

- The group is accountable as a unit.

The more these conditions are true, the more benefits the team can expect to realize from a team development process.

Individual Accountability Versus Teamwork: Stages or Steps in the Process

A well-designed development process will guide the group through the stages of team development more easily. Figure 4.1 illustrates the classical stages—forming, storming, norming, performing—that most groups experience on the way to becoming a high-performing team.

During the forming stage, team members wonder, "How do I fit in? What is expected of me?" At this stage, the team needs direction and clarity of purpose.

The second stage, storming, typically occurs when conflict about values begins and leadership may be questioned. The team members most need role clarification and agreement on a code of conduct. This is the stage when I am frequently called in to "fix" the group and to help people "to get along better."

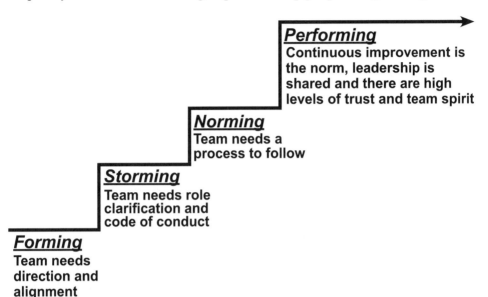

Performing
Continuous improvement is the norm, leadership is shared and there are high levels of trust and team spirit

Norming
Team needs a process to follow

Storming
Team needs role clarification and code of conduct

Forming
Team needs direction and alignment

Adapted from "Development Sequence in Small Groups" B. W. Tuckman 1955
Stages of Team Development
Figure 4.1

In the norming stage, the team begins to discover how to work together. Leadership consults with the team, and the team benefits most by having a process to follow. In this stage, I find most teams discontinue their team-building efforts. They feel content that they are finally working better together and relieved to be past the storming stage.

Few achieve the final stage, performing. Team members must have patience and expend consistent effort to reach and sustain this level. This stage is the ultimate goal because it is truly the breakthrough level where continuous improvement becomes the norm, and team members share leadership. High levels of trust and team spirit characterize the team.

Developing Extraordinary Teams

Rarely do organizations have the internal capacity to launch and sustain a team development initiative; this is particularly true with senior teams, but a qualified external facilitator can assure an effective implementation. Otherwise, it can feel like attempting to perform your own appendectomy! Whether you do it yourself or contract with a qualified individual, all teams can benefit from team development, provided they meet the conditions mentioned earlier in this key.

The multi-step Team Development Process™ (TDP) that my colleagues and I facilitate focuses on teaching individuals to work together as a team. TDP helps teams in the following twelve ways:

1. **Develop a process that increases knowledge, understanding, acceptance,** and behavioral skills to create a climate of inclusion and acceptance, since enhancing trust-building skills is a major learning point. A qualified facilitator will assure that each team member is included in the process. Before the TDP is complete, team members will begin to realize the significant benefits that come for having everyone involved and included. Prior to a TDP experience, many team members may feel reluctant to become involved because the climate is dominated by those who are unaware of their behavior and the consequences.

2. **Increase each team member's personal contribution to the team climate and level of trust.** The learning that occurs during TDP creates awareness of each members' behavior and the impact it has on the team climate. Thus, the level of trust can be enhanced as team members develop new behavioral skills through the process.

3. **Build each team member's capacity to increase their contribution to the team results** by sharpening the focus on the team's purpose and goals.

4. **Provide a 360-degree feedback about each team member's contribution,** based on what each member observes within the team. This type of feedback provides a real-time snapshot of what is going on within the team in terms of meaningful, task-focused contributions to team goals.

5. **Develop action plans to achieve the next level of performance** by clarifying the gap between where the team's performance is currently compared to where the members want it to be. For example, how far has the team moved toward achieving the performance challenge or objectives?

6. **Determine next steps for increasing the team's alignment to**

the vision. By illustrating the degree of alignment among team members, an action plan can be developed to uncover those areas where the team lacks alignment, the causes, and actions to remedy any lack. Many times, the TDP experience creates the opportunity for those causes to be identified and resolved.

7. **Reaffirm commitments to increase trust.** When team members realize that TDP is a "process" and not simply an "event," they realize that they will become accountable to each other for their commitments to change their behavior.

8. **Increase listening skills and listening adaptability among team members.** A highly qualified TDP facilitator will provide exercises that result in enhanced listening skills and illustrate alternate forms of listening that will be more effective with more people in more situations.

9. **Build effective communication among team members** by increasing awareness of each individual's preferred way of receiving information. With intent to develop the highest levels of communication effectiveness, members learn how to communicate in ways that works best for each person.

10. **Identify individual strengths and areas for improvement** through personal assessments, survey and group feedback that point out areas for reinforcement and development.

11. **Build a communication action plan** to ensure that all stakeholders are informed of any strategic changes that will affect them and to provide for stakeholders' input before changes are implemented. This step results in maximum buy-in and reduced resistance.

12. **Identify unmet work expectations on the team and establish priorities** to meet those expectations. Everyone's expectations about their workplace extend beyond merely being paid. At any given time, expectations may be met or unmet, spoken or unspoken. The TDP includes a questionnaire to identify expectations and strategies that will help get team members to communicate their expectations, even if they cannot currently be met in the workplace.

TDP begins with completion of the Team Alignment Questionnaire (TAQ) described earlier in this Key and in Key One. The TAQ is also administered periodically to measure the team's progress.

Shared Leadership

An effective team development program must address the subject of leadership. Traditionally, managers have acted as if they had all the answers and created a control-based workplace as described in Key One. They believed they could simply announce a project, delegate it, and watch it be accomplished. That type of leadership role has totally dissolved with the introduction of the information age, the current shift to the Conceptual Age, and the demand for Top Talent.

In the old model of leadership, one leader headed up the team, whose members were all followers. Today, with flatter organizations and self-managed teams, leadership is not a role…it is an *act*, or a *behavior*! An organization that shares leadership encourages employees to perform "acts of leadership," that is, to look for ways in which they can make a contribution outside the specific role. In shared leadership, everyone on the team—regardless of role, position or title—performs acts of influence. Willingly shared leadership practiced by all members of a team results in the ultimate level of team development and individual performance. This is the performing stage of the model described earlier in this key.

Shared leadership simply expands the definition of leadership to include anyone and everyone who chooses to perform an act of leadership. In an accountability-based workplace which has high levels of trust, anyone can influence others in the organization to take notice and act.

Innovation

In high performance team environment, creativity and innovation flourish, and the organization gets the very best Top Talent has to offer. Remember, a breakthrough idea can come from anywhere in the organization when Top Talent fill every position. One shining example is a not-for-profit client whose custodian, after listening to a Yanni CD, suggested that the organization bring Yanni to town for their annual fundraiser, long before anyone here had ever heard of Yanni. That proved to be one of their most successful fundraisers.

Another great example of creativity and innovation occurred at a Verizon call center. A customer service representative contributed the idea for an extremely successful marketing campaign after she purchased a phone line for her teenage daughter as a birthday gift when the rep grew tired of having the family phone tied up continually. You may remember that campaign promoting separate phone lines for teenagers.

When team members are committed to achieving shared objectives, everyone can become their best. In an accountability-driven, values-based work place, management trusts workers to be great and believes that everyone really wants to do their best work. Those who can't be trusted simply can't stay.

This leadership approach allows people to set their own goals and become personally responsible. The formal leader really takes on the role of coach and mentor. I will address coaching and mentoring in Key Six and discuss the skills required to effectively operate with this form of leadership.

Key Points

→ The senior team must guide the process by becoming a model team and develop an action plan to establish a responsibility-based culture.

→ The beginning point is bench-marking the level of team alignment and trust with the Team Alignment Questionnaire™.

→ The senior leadership team experiences unique challenges because membership in the senior team is a part-time role.

→ A real team is a small number of people with complementary skills who are committed to a common purpose, performance goals, and approach for which they hold themselves mutually accountable.

→ A high-performance team meets all the conditions of a real team and also has members who are deeply committed to one another's personal growth and success.

→ Many groups may call themselves a team but may lack one or more elements required to be a real team.

→ The four types of teams or groups that benefit from team development include:

1. Project teams can get results twice as quickly with a formalized team development process.

2. Quality teams can create more balance by measuring team member roles and implementing a process to develop and fully utilize everyone's innovative skills.

3. Work teams, groups of people who work together every day, can significantly improve their output by taking time out to clarify and reach agreement on their purpose, vision, values and goals.

4. Senior management teams need a process that will align team members, remove the politics, and achieve the results they know are possible.

➤ There are four classical stages or phases in team development: forming, storming, norming, and performing. In my experience, most teams call for help in the storming stage and believe they have "arrived" when they reach the norming stage and may never truly become high-performing.

➤ All teams can benefit from the Team Development Process™ (TDP).

➤ In an extraordinary team, leadership is not a role…it is an act, or a behavior with high levels of trust where anyone can influence others to take notice and act.

➤ Breakthrough ideas can come from anywhere when Top Talent fill every position.

Questions to Ponder

1. How important is it to you to achieve innovative breakthroughs that will provide added value to all stakeholders?

2. How many teams within your company are "real" teams?

3. How well are members of the senior team handling their "part-timer" role?

4. What stages of development can you identify among the team within your company?

5. What is the most significant benefit you and your teams could realize by implementing a team development process?

TABS Action Plan

T. What was the main **thing** you got from this key?

A. What **action** are you willing to take?

B. What **benefit** do you expect to get from it?

S. What is the **single step** you will take to **get started** within 48 hours?

Assignments

- Consider taking your team through the Team Alignment Questionnaire™ to measure the levels of alignment and trust.

- Determine the groups or pseudo-teams that need to become real teams.

- Have all groups or teams that think they are "real" teams define their compelling performance challenge.

KEY FIVE

A CULTURE OF CONTINUOUS LEARNING:

MASTERING THE ESSENTIAL SKILLS

> "In the long run, the only sustainable source of competitive advantage is your organization's ability to learn faster than its competition."
>
> **- Peter Senge, *The Fifth Discipline***

A CULTURE OF CONTINUOUS LEARNING

L earning is far more than simply acquiring information; it is the expansion of our ability to produce the results we want in life. Turning good people into Top Talent includes a culture of continuous learning to fully develop the skills and abilities each job requires for masterful performance.

It used to take seven to fourteen years for fifty percent of a worker's technical skills to become obsolete; now it takes just three to five years. This investment in human capital is an asset, not a cost. How well are your training and development processes aligned with your strategy? Are you adequately prepared to develop the talent within your organization, both now and in the future?

Training Pays Dividends for Employees and Investors

The results of a major training practices and outcomes study conducted by the American Society for Training & Development (ASTD) found definitive evidence that investments in workforce training can predict a company's future financial performance, including its total stockholder return (TSR). Companies that invested $680 per employee more in training than the average company improved their TSR the next year by six percentage points, even after considering other factors. Companies in the top half of the study group had an average TSR the following year of 36.9%, while firms in the bottom half had an average TSR of only 19.8%. For comparison purposes, the Standard & Poor 500 had an annual return of 25.5% during the same period. Thus, firms in the top half had a TSR that was 86% higher than firms in the bottom half, and a 45% higher TSR than the market average.

"It is clear that a firm's commitment to workplace learning is directly linked to its bottom line—and investors. Wall Street, and financial analysts should pay attention," says Mark Van Buren, Research Director for ASTD. "Knowing a firm's education and training investment improves the power to predict its future TSR by 50 percent. This information is powerful—investors and companies will both benefit by tracking and reporting on training expenditures," he emphasizes.

ASTD researchers also found a similar pattern with gross profit margin, income per employee, and price-to-book ratios. Firms in the top quarter of the study group who invested $1,595 per employee in training experienced 24% higher gross profit margins, 218% higher revenue per employee, and 26% higher price-to-book ratios than firms in the bottom quarter that invested only $128 per employee.

Essential Skills

Essential skills are the multipliers of job performance. Personal skills, behaviors, and attributes were once referred to as "soft" skills, but are now widely recognized as the critical difference that allows Top Talent to outperform average workers exponentially.

Job skills are a combination of functional, technical, and essential skills. Each job has a unique requirement for these combined skills that makes superior job performance possible. At one time, workers were hired primarily for their technical skills and not much attention was given to the "soft" skills. In Key Seven, I will discuss how these essential skills and attributes can be measured and related to specific job requirements.

Let's take a closer look at the essential skill called *interpersonal skills*. The results from interviews conducted by Computer Technology Industry Association (CompTIA) of 501 CIO's and HR managers at companies with revenues of $20 million or greater indicate that CIO's value soft skills such as communications and patience, while HR professionals tend to screen candidates for hard, technical skills.

In a 2001 survey, management consultants Towers Perrin found 66% of North American companies reported that their focus in 1998 was exclusively on financial results when assessing employee performance. At the time of the survey, that group was projected to shrink to 16% by 2004 as greater attention was paid to softer skills. How can we account for this 50% shift in emphasis from an area that traditionally considered technical know-how essential?

A survey conducted by an independent research firm involving responses from 1,400 CFOs from a stratified random sample of U.S. companies with more than 20 employees reported in October 2001, that being able to "work well with others" tops the list of CFOs' "must haves." In another survey, 26% of CFOs polled said interpersonal skills are the most important consideration when hiring senior-level employees. Companies are looking for persuasive communicators who can lead and motivate others.

Consider how important the following skills and attributes are for key jobs in *your* company:

- Striving for self-awareness

- Demonstrating sincere interest in others

- Treating all people with respect, courtesy, and consideration

- Respecting differences in the attitudes and perspectives of others

- Listening, observing, and striving to gain understanding of others

- Communicating effectively

How much performance leverage do you think these skills provide?

Emotional Intelligence

Daniel Goleman and his colleagues, in their classic book, *Primal Leadership*, refer to these essential skills as emotional intelligence (EQ). They divide these EQ competencies into two categories: personal competence—how we manage ourselves, including self-awareness—and social competence—how we manage relationships, including social awareness.

Goleman and his colleagues consider these competencies to apply universally to any person in any job but most critical for leadership and management positions. They have conducted research which clearly indicates that these skills directly influence management effectiveness. The level of emotional intelligence within the executive team is directly linked to performance and productivity throughout the organization.

More Important Than IQ

A person's ability to manage him or herself and relate to other people matters twice as much as IQ or technical skills in job success. In his research, Goleman discovered that emotional intelligence plays an important role in surprising places, such as computer programming. Studies found that the top 10% of performers in EQ exceeded average performers in producing effective programs by 320%. The superstars at the 1% level produced an amazing 1,272% more than average.

Solid research proves that the skills that contribute to emotional intelligence can be measured and learned. In fact, many of these skills *must* be learned because they do not naturally occur and rarely appear in the traditional education system's curriculum. While the good news is that essential skills can be learned, the bad news is it takes longer and requires a different process than learning technical or functional skills.

Thinking Brain Versus Emotional Brain

Most training programs for enhancing skills are designed for cognitive learning. Cognitive learning targets the neo-cortex, the "thinking brain." This method can be effective for learning technical and functional skills, but it is often event-based and short term in nature, lacking in application, accountability, and measurement.

Emotional intelligence abilities—such as the personal skills—target the limbic or "emotional brain." Reeducating the emotional brain requires a lot of practice and repetition.

Goleman concluded that emotional intelligence skills develop only with a sincere desire and concerted effort. He claims, "A brief seminar won't help, and it can't be learned through a how-to manual. The thinking brain can comprehend something after a single hearing or reading. The limbic brain, on the other hand, is a much slower learner—particularly when the challenge is to relearn deeply ingrained habits. The brain must literally be rewired to work differently and that does not happen in a series of loosely connected training events."

Ten Best Practices for Mastery of Essential Skills

Essential skills are those practices considered critical to the effectiveness of a particular role or position. Each position carries its own particular accountabilities or reason it exists, and best practices for learning must include a clear definition of those job accountabilities and the skills required to accomplish them.

Many people are placed in positions because of the technical skill they demonstrated in a prior position, but those same technical skills become obsolete in the new position and are no longer relevant to achieving the accountabilities of the job. However, it is the personal skills, or soft skills—the emotional intelligence—that will most determine their effectiveness.

Applying the following ten elements will ensure that learning is focused on mastery of those essential skills necessary to accomplish the learner's job accountabilities:

1. Engaging the participant's manager to fully sponsor the learning process

2. Assessing current skills and knowledge levels of the specific area of learning

3. Jump-starting the learning process through self-discovery such as online or web-based learning

4. Interacting, discussing, and practicing the new skill in a workshop-type environment to develop personal skills

5. Reinforcing the workshop experience with additional web-based learning

6. Personal coaching to assure development and application of action plans

7. Evaluating to measure learning effectiveness (relevance and application of new learning)

8. Assessing final skills and retention level of what was learned

9. Managers teaching and coaching their direct reports using what they have just learned

10. The final element of best practices is for management to reinforce the new skills. The manager must become the coach of the learner back on the job to ensure relevant use of the new learning. This can be as simple as an acknowledgement that the individual has used the new skill or calling attention to the fact that a particular result was achieved when the new skill was used.

Personal Mastery

George Leonard, author of *Mastery*, calls continuous learning the key to success and long-term fulfillment. He says that mastery is not perfection, but rather a journey. Leonard, an expert in the martial arts, points out that the masters of the martial arts cannot tell their students when they will get their black belt because that happens only when the student is ready. You don't know you're ready until you are there.

Leonard also makes the point that, first, attaining mastery requires the willingness to try and fail, and try again. The second requirement is contentment on the plateau between learning cycles. Learning, after all, is not a continuous line straight up. To achieve mastery, the learning must keep going through the boredom of what seems to be limited progress, maintaining the momentum to achieve the breakthrough to mastery. Remember, the journey toward mastery begins by being good at what you do, combined with a desire to be the best.

Personal mastery is the ultimate level of skill development, and requires the discipline to focus effort, time, and resources while patiently moving toward the learning objective. The essential cornerstone of an organization with a culture of continuous learning is individual commitment to personal mastery. An organization's capacity for learning is no greater than the sum of its members.

The Cycle of Mastery™

The Cycle of Mastery™ (Figure 5.1)—an integral part of The Effectiveness Coach® Approach and The Effectiveness Learning Process™—illustrates the concept of continuous learning involved in turning good people into Top Talent.

You cannot improve what you don't know. The Cycle of Mastery begins by creating *awareness* through personal assessments. When you become aware of your behavior—what you are doing or not doing relative to an expectation or standard—it becomes more likely that you can improve. Unless I realize that my behavior—something I say or how I say it—has a negative impact on another person, causing them to withdraw and withhold information, I am not likely to change that behavior.

Next is *discovery*—determining the relevance of these insights so that you may apply them. One of my clients recently remarked that he had become aware that he had poor listening skills because he lacked patience when someone interrupted him while he performed a task. During our coaching call, I asked a few questions to determine the reason for his impatience. It turned out that he had an open door policy, so anyone could walk in at any time and interrupt him. When his boundaries were breached, he grew irritated and really did not want to hear what the visitor had to say. He realized how costly this habit was and that there were benefits to listening, despite his irritation at the interruption. Now he feels motivated to apply this discovery, which is the next step in the Cycle.

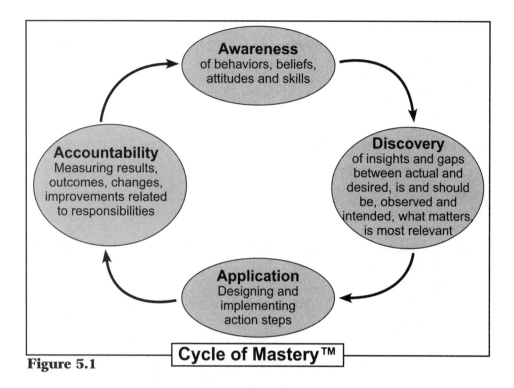

Figure 5.1   **Cycle of Mastery™**

It is important to know what actions you will take so that there is follow-through rather than just an "Aha!" moment. When my client understood the relevance of his discovery, he committed to taking actions that would apply this new information, determining first that he would create the appropriate climate for effective listening to occur. He began by modifying his "open door" policy to mean open by invitation and with sufficient notice. He is still available, just not instantly. By arranging a time to discuss issues and concerns, his staff knows that they will have his undivided attention throughout the time both have agreed to. They get the time and opportunity to be heard; he gets the ideas and input he wants to achieve a more significant result.

As we have discussed in this example, the application phase of the cycle is focused on results; this leads to personal accountability. With new awareness, discovery, and application, what results can you measure? How do these results relate to what you are expected to accomplish and the job accountabilities you have agreed to achieve? Since my client in this example is a senior executive with his company, developing talented people is one of his major accountabilities, and he is now able to connect his need to develop his listening skills to his accountabilities.

Each time I realize that a gap exists between my current practice of a skill that is related to one or more of my accountabilities, a new learning experience can occur that continues the cycle. Each "revolution" of the cycle can take me higher in the development of my personal and professional skills. When appropriately connected to my accountabilities, each new learning experience will create greater results.

Factors Influencing Learning Effectiveness

In order to make the shift from event-based learning, which tends to have limited usefulness in increasing skills, to a culture of continuous learning, each of the following roles must be considered:

1. **Participant's Manager:** The number one influence on learning effectiveness is how well the manager prepares the participant prior to launching the learning process. How many times have you been part of a training experience that launched when you received a memo telling you to show up at a certain time and place? Participants are more likely to attend with a positive frame of mind and greater eagerness to learn when their managers prepare them for the learning experience by communicating its importance and relevance to the participants' jobs. How well the manager reinforces the learning during and following the learning process is also a major influence on the outcome. Likewise, when the participant returns from a learning experience, the manager can reinforce the learning by scheduling time for a debriefing session. Together, the manager and participants can determine how the learning applies to the job.

2. **Participant**: Obviously, the participants have an effect on their own learning based on what they do prior to, during, and after the learning process. The most effective learning process uses some form of pre-work in addition to the event or classroom experience. Follow-up personal coaching with on-line, or other self-paced reinforcement will strengthen the results. Coach-based learning is critical for mastering essential skills. Ideally, the manager is a coach-based manager which I will discuss further in Key Six.

3. **Instructor/Facilitator:** The instructor plays a significant role throughout the process—not just during direct interaction with

participants. The instructor must coach the participants' manager to communicate the importance and expected results of the learning before attendance. The instructor should also provide guidance for the reinforcement and follow-though participants receive after attendance at the learning experience.

Measuring Learning Effectiveness

The direct results of effective learning can be seen in any industry in which the training has taken place. In sales, for example, you'll see increased sales volume, greater customer retention, shortened sales cycles, improved closing ratios and higher profit per sale. In customer service, training will generate a reduction in repeat calls to the help desk; reduced time to complete reports, forms, or tasks; an increased volume of calls with comparable qualitative measures; reduced hold time; and fewer calls in the queue.

Leadership Selection and Development Practices

Vital Learning Corporation, which I am affiliated with, recently surveyed more than 300 executives across America on corporate leadership selection and development practices. The survey revealed:

- Less than half of the organizations surveyed said that they identify high-performing employees and aggressively manage their development as leaders.

- About one third of the respondents reported their companies have programs and processes in place to develop leaders.

- Nearly half of organizations surveyed reported that their senior management does not take the actions necessary to develop leaders, although they claim they do or believe it is important.

Keys to Improving Leadership Effectiveness: A Learning Process

Leadership development is designed to change leadership behavior, so business results can be improved. Most management and leadership trainings are events...two to five days with minimal or no follow-up. Typically, the participants decide whether they actually use what they have learned or not! With so much being invested in leadership training, what is missing?

Rigorous research shows that it is impossible to learn to be a more effective leader as a result of a single learning event. As stated in Daniel Goleman's research cited earlier in this key, changing behavior takes time. Leadership development must change behavior for business results to improve so the organization can be a winning company. Only a process of continuous development—a series of events with application and reinforcement that includes most or all of the 10 best practices mentioned previously—can achieve lasting change in leadership behavior.

Assessment-Based

The need for accurate and timely assessment of training and development priorities has never been more important than in today's rapidly growing workplace. In my leadership development work, I use the Leadership Competency Assessment™ (LCA) which measures observed skill levels from the perspectives of self, boss, peers, subordinates and customers or others with whom the individual interacts frequently.

The 50 leadership competencies are organized in ten categories:

1. Communication Skills
2. Self-Awareness
3. Managing Change
4. Personal Responsibility
5. Interpersonal Skills
6. Managing Own Performance
7. Managing Differences
8. Managing Others Performance
9. Managing Innovation
10. Leadership

Learning Benchmark

The results of the initial LCA establish the learning benchmark prior to the implementation of the Leadership Development Process™ (LDP). LDP is a five module (ten-unit) curriculum that is typically implemented over 12 to 18 months with reassessments along the way. The following modules are designed to address each of the ten skill areas measured by the LCA

- Module 1: Increasing Leadership Impact

- Module 2: Improving People Skills

- Module 3: Increasing Engagement and Commitment

- Module 4: Building a High Performing Team

- Module 5: Developing Shared Leadership Skills

A Leadership Effectiveness Case Study

In 1998, a leading global medical diagnostics equipment company contacted my colleague, Jeff Taylor of R. C. Taylor and Associates, a fellow affiliate of Integro Leadership Institute. With a technical assistance center (TAC) that had the lowest customer satisfaction ratings in the industry, the company wanted to develop and launch a customer service training initiative for its TAC. The TAC plays a key role in the company's success by assisting clients in pathology labs with technical questions or problems related to use of their equipment and consumables. They called the initiative "Leap of Excellence" and determined such goals as:

- Drive a culture change from a technical focus to a customer focus.

- Make their TAC the best in the industry.

- Empower individuals to do whatever it takes to totally delight the customer.

- Assure that the TAC becomes a competitive advantage in the selling process.

- Drive personal and professional success for all individuals.

The customer service training program has evolved into what is now called Customer Excellence Optimization (CEO) with the theme, "If better is possible, then good is not enough…it's all about raising the bar." The focus was—and continues to be—on personal excellence and accountability.

The cumulative impact of individual excellence has resulted in sustained customer service excellence, with the TAC going from last place in the industry to #1, according to external customer surveys. They also became the leading global diagnostics company in both sales and service in 2002.

As a result of the leadership and team development processes that were implemented simultaneously and continue within the organization, the company experienced documented growth and sustained excellence from 1998 through the first quarter of 2004.

In addition to the satisfaction survey statistics as shown in Figure 5.2, the TAC is experiencing:

- Record high numbers of customer calls.

- Their lowest staffing level ever.

- Steady or improved quality issues.

- Increased turnover due to individuals successfully marketing themselves for higher level positions in the company.

- Downsizings, reorganizations, consolidations and management change in the TAC.

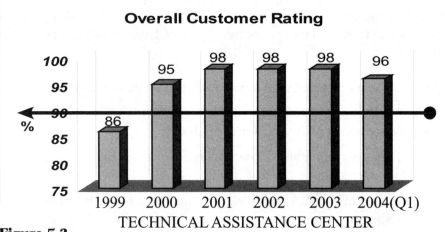

Figure 5.2

The keys to the success of this initiative are:

- Commitment from the top of the TAC down.

- Recognition that a culture change is required.

- A process-driven approach with benchmarks.

- Establishment of shared leadership, empowerment, and accountability at all levels.

- Management's willingness to change processes and metrics to align the new culture.

- Providing on-going training tools, resources, and support at all levels of the organization.

- Celebrating success but never becoming complacent.

- Willingness of individuals to embrace the culture change and hold themselves accountable to keep it alive.

- Remaining centered and focused on their purpose and passion through changes and challenges.

R.C. Taylor's account representative for this company reminds us that continued excellence requires continual vigilance—an ongoing process of learning—to keep everyone focused on the goals. She says, "It is easy to become complacent, and in times of stress, it is easy to slip back into old behavior patterns."

Where to Begin?

As with any organizational change or cultural shift initiative, the top is always the place to begin—with the leadership. Leadership affects everything! Leadership's behavior creates the culture or climate employees work in, and employees' attitudes are affected by their perception of that culture. It takes Top Talent to improve productivity, maximize competitive advantage, and achieve the organization's vision and purpose, but unless an organization has a reputation as a great place to work, it will not attract Top Talent. Top Talent simply will not perform in an environment that they perceive as negative.

Executive Attention Required

To achieve a compelling vision and become a winning company, leaders must focus learning initiatives on making improvements that will enhance business performance—such as customer loyalty, product quality and innovation, speed of development and delivery, and sales effectiveness. You must have employees with the right skills to meet the strategic challenges of the organization. Implementing career development and talent management strategies that keep high-potential and high-performing employees engaged is essential. Leaders must take the initiative to identify development needs and opportunities, and create a culture of continuous learning.

It is essential to establish an environment where workers feel they make a difference, are valued, and are able to continually learn new skills. By capturing the hearts and minds of their employees, organizations can expect to have people who will create, innovate, and more quickly move the organization forward to achieve its vision. When this happens, your organization will be well on its way to turning good people into Top Talent and maximizing your competitive advantage.

In the next key you will discover the critical key, Coach Based Management: Maximizing Worker-Manager Contribution.

Key Points

→ Learning is defined as expanding the ability to produce the results that we want in life. Thus, learning is more than simply acquiring more information.

→ Essential skills are particular behaviors and attributes that determine the capacity to apply the specific technical skills of the job. Today, soft skills have become essential skills.

→ To be successful in a position or career, one must master three different skill sets:

1. Job Skills

2. Functional Skills

3. Personal Skills

→ The reality is that essential (soft) personal skills have a greater effect on performance than technical or functional skills.

→ The research is also very clear that essential skills require considerable habit change, unlearning, and relearning. The brain must literally be rewired to work differently and that simply does not happen in a series of loosely connected training events.

→ Personal mastery is the discipline of continually clarifying and deepening our personal vision and focusing our energies. This ultimate level of skill development results from an individual's commitment to becoming the best and the willingness to focus his or her effort, time, and resources.

→ The Cycle of Mastery™ illustrates the concept of ongoing learning, a continuous process that begins with awareness, moves on to discovery of what's relevant, then to implementation and execution, and finally, to a focus on results leading to accountability.

➤ Creating a learning culture involves a shift to a culture that supports an on-going process of learning that is application-driven and focused on results rather than actions.

➤ The involvement of the participant's manager before the launch is the number one influence on the effectiveness of the learning process.

➤ When leaders take the initiative to identify development needs and opportunities, workers feel they make a difference, are valued, and are able to continually learn new skills.

➤ A global medical diagnostic company has had documented growth and sustained excellence since 1998 when they simultaneously implemented the leadership and team development processes.

Questions to Ponder

1. How important is it to you for key people to maximize the essential skills?

2. In your organization, how balanced is the emphasis placed on technical know-how (hard skills) and the essential (soft personal skills) for key positions?

3. How committed and skilled are your managers to actively sponsor learning processes by communicating their importance and value to their staff?

4. How effectively are managers in your organization reinforcing and following up on the learning processes that their staff attends?

5. What benefits could you realize by measuring the effectiveness of your organization's learning process?

TABS Action Plan

T. What was the main **thing** you got from this key?

A. What **action** are you willing to take?

B. What **benefit** do you expect to get from it?

S. What is the **single step** you will take to **get started** within 48 hours?

Assignments

- Identify the positions that may have significant skill gaps between how key jobs are being done and how they *need* to be done.

- Determine how effectively all managers (beginning at the top) function as an active sponsor of learning by communicating the importance and value of the learning their staff receives.

- Create a task force that will recommend improvements to the learning process by shifting the focus away from events.

- Investigate the implementation of a process that will establish a culture of continuous learning for all key positions including the creation of a Chief Learning Officer position, unless you already have one.

KEY  SIX

COACH-BASED MANAGEMENT:

MAXIMIZING WORKER AND MANAGER CONTRIBUTION

"To turn good people into Top Talent, managers must replace typical management activities like supervising, checking, monitoring, and controlling with new behaviors like masterful coaching and effective communicating."

- Bob Moore, The Effectiveness Coach®

COACH-BASED MANAGEMENT

If we agree that organizations rise or fall depending on how effectively they utilize people, then we must recognize that the manager plays a critical role in turning good people into Top Talent. A coach-based relationship is the ideal way to maximize worker and manager contributions to organizational results.

Knowledge Workers

During the early days of the industrial revolution, getting work done was based on managers having all the answers and telling everyone what to do. The late Peter Drucker warned us back in 1966 in his best seller *The Effective Executive* that a time was coming when the workforce would consist primarily of knowledge workers and that we would not know how to manage them.

That time is now. We now realize that today's knowledge workers expect to achieve personal fulfillment on the job and want to be mentored and coached to fully develop their talents. The great news is this new kind of worker brings added capacity to the organization.

John Naisbitt, in his best seller *Megatrends*, published in 1982, reported the beginning of the transformation of the U.S. workplace into a place where the manager creates a nourishing environment for personal growth. He predicted that increasingly we will think of managers as teachers, mentors, and developers of human potential. Naisbitt asserted, "The challenge will be to retrain *managers*, not workers, for the reinvented, information-age corporation."

Daniel Pink in his book *A Whole New Mind: Moving from the Information Age to the Conceptual Age* asserts that there must be a shift away from left

113

brain to right brain thinking. This will require both worker and manager to seek more balance in their approach to everything including how they communicate, solve problems and create new solutions for an ever changing market place.

Management Responsibilities

In my 35 years of experience working with a variety of organizations, I've rarely heard a manager say, "It is my responsibility to facilitate (which Webster defines as 'to make easier or less difficult') the worker's performance on the job." What do managers perceive their responsibilities to be? Clearly, most managers see themselves as responsible for performance and outcomes, yet they are ill-equipped when it comes to knowing the best ways to achieve those results with today's worker.

Traditional Beliefs About Managing

Let's first examine some of the beliefs about being a boss that managers bring to the job. I distinctly remember wanting to become a manager because I believed I would be more effective than my manager was. At the time, I never considered all that being the boss would do for my ego.

What about the managers in your organization? To what extent have their egos become attached to their role of boss, being in charge and having authority and power?

Many managers believe as I did, that they have paid their dues. We believe our time has come to control others. Unconsciously, we tend to develop habits, behaviors, and attitudes that reinforce that our boss approach is the right way, maybe the only way.

Moore's Top Ten Management Myths

Here are "Moore's Top Ten" beliefs and attitudes that managers tend to adopt to support their approach to managing, which may diminish their effectiveness as leaders:

1. My job is to push for results.

2. Any techniques to accomplish results, including directing, lecturing, and various forms of intimidation, are proper.

3. It is my right to keep secrets about certain rules, policies, objectives, and expectations.

4. I must always appear to have the answers and to be right about everything.

5. It is my job to inspect, observe, and check up on everything.

6. Decisions about what information is shared with whom and when will occur at my discretion.

7. It is my responsibility to point out mistakes and errors as soon as I discover them.

8. As the boss, I make all the decisions, solve all the problems, and come up with all the elements of any new plans and procedures.

9. My primary reason for being at this organization is to ensure that we achieve bottom line results.

10. Unless workers are told what to do and are closely monitored, results will be inadequate or substandard.

The Manager-Coach

Many predict that the title "manager" will disappear sometime during the first half of the twenty-first century. What do you think the new name for the role we now call a manager will be? My recommendation is "coach."

Unfortunately, most managers are very ineffective coaches. Surveys by Smart & Associates, conducted over the past 20 years, indicate that 75% of employees rate their managers as only "fair" or "poor" in coaching skills.

Manager Accountabilities for Contribution

The increasing demands of business require managers at all levels to expand the scope of their responsibility and personal accountabilities. As the manager's role changes, so must the manager. Today's business climate and marketplace have become increasingly competitive and fast-paced. It is essential for organizations to work with speed and precision to enable people in key positions to achieve their critical accountabilities and objectives.

Consider the following five managerial challenges or key accountabilities of the job of manager:

1. To improve one's personal performance and results

2. To effectively manage both human and physical assets

3. To ensure that the work atmosphere is cooperative, non-threatening, and supportive

4. To be seen as a leader by all employees

5. To develop a participatory management style that is open, flexible and inclusive

The common thread throughout these accountabilities is the consideration of the human (intrinsic) side of the equation, not just the results (extrinsic) or the procedures and rules (systemic) to follow to achieve them.

Measuring Management's Contribution

Coach-based management centers on the concept that the new, high-tech, global economy of the 21st century requires more from managers than ever before. Management accountabilities and manager contribution to organizational results have changed dramatically. Managers at all levels are expected to accomplish more results faster and with fewer resources for a more demanding customer.

Continuously assessing a manager's present level of effectiveness and the degree to which he or she achieves all the accountabilities of a coach-based manager is critical for maximum contribution. Even managers who are effective coaches must have a means of determining their strengths and weaknesses. I recommend a manager diagnostic system with questions tailored to include a balanced mix of job skills, functional skills, and interpersonal skills.

The Effectiveness Coach® Approach utilizes the Manager Contribution Assessment™, a tool that evaluates how well a manager performs based on input from multiple respondents (self, direct reports, peers, manager, and others). The respondents consider the three skills or capacities associated with each the five management challenges or accountabilities. For example, within the accountability "Employee Support," respondents are asked to answer a series of questions related to the following skills:

- Employee dialogue regarding performance related to their job profile and mutually agreed upon goals with a view toward helping them to improve

- Employee coaching to improve performance or make the appropriate changes in a timely manner

- Employee partnering to develop loyalty and trust

The assessment process creates awareness that leads to discoveries and can result in actions that enhance results and accountabilities. For executives who utilize external coaches, an assessment can determine the skill gaps that need the most attention as well as the strengths to be reinforced.

Management Effectiveness

The survey conducted by Vital Learning Corporation, mentioned in Key Five, revealed that the organizations surveyed do not give themselves high marks at developing leaders. More than 70% reported that their supervisors and managers do not have the skills to develop the capabilities of their direct reports. Since over 50% of most on-the-job training occurs between supervisor and employee, unless supervisors do it, it won't get done.

The survey further revealed that six in ten leaders are not effective at communicating expectations to their direct reports. Effective management is proven to yield greater customer satisfaction and higher profits. Data from other research has shown leaders rated in the top 20% of leadership effectiveness in a large high tech company achieved 39% more customer satisfaction than those in the middle 60%, and 74% more than those in the bottom 20%. Other data demonstrates that in a large mortgage bank leaders rated in the top 10% of leadership effectiveness attained 89% more net income than those in the middle 80%.

Ten Reasons to Adopt Coach-Based Management

1. Downsizing and outsourcing have changed the organizational structure and workers' roles, creating a new approach to working with people to achieve business results.

2. The pace of business has changed; results must happen faster.

3. Business is global, and there is a need for greater inclusion and valuing of diversity in order for businesses to be competitive.

4. Coaching helps eliminate a culture of fear and paternalism, which can escalate during periods of rapid change.

5. Technology no longer provides a competitive advantage—talented people do.

6. Being an employer of choice that attracts and retains Top Talent is no longer optional; it has become *essential*.

7. The employment contract has changed, and individuals are now more responsible for managing their own development and career advancement.

8. Many management styles, skills, strategies, and techniques are no longer effective with today's worker, which makes an immediate shift to coach-based management essential.

9. With the technological explosion and the rate of obsolescence of learning, organizations now require new information more often than ever before.

10. As Peter Drucker and John Naisbitt predicted, the information age has produced workers who require a different style of management and workplace in order to fully utilize their talents. Daniel Pink's assertions that a shift is underway to the Conceptual Age add additional compelling reasons to manage differently—not just better.

The Shift to Coach-Based Management

The shift to coach-based management begins with the premise that we must have an abiding faith and trust in people's desire to be great. The most effective coaching comes about when people *ask* to be coached. For this to occur, the coach-based manager must focus attention on the following five areas:

1. Establish a Safe Environment

The manager/coach must first create an environment that assures a level of trust in which an open and straightforward dialogue can occur. The manager/coach must demonstrate an attitude of respect for the worker's good intentions, regardless of actual performance.

2. Provide Specific Feedback

The most effective feedback directly addresses the specific gap in performance and how actual results differ from expectations, standards, or goals.

3. Share Responsibility for Creating Dialogue

Both the coach and the worker must share ownership of the performance gap. This is best achieved when both agree to listen with the intention of being mutually understood and to allow themselves to be influenced by the other.

4. Create Awareness That Can Lead to Positive Action

Performance gaps often result from the worker's false assumptions about what results are possible, and his or her ability to perform the job. Awareness of these assumptions can be the first step toward increased self-motivation and positive actions.

5. Leverage Strengths

When the manager/coach builds on the worker's unique strengths, he or she creates powerful leverage to improve performance by fully utilizing the worker's talents and strengths.

With this framework of faith and trust in place, when the opportunity for coaching presents itself, both the worker (coachee) and manager (coach) will recognize it and make full use of it.

A Stretch for Many Managers

Becoming an effective coach-based manager requires a stretch for many managers and a major shift from the role of an autocratic boss or demanding supervisor. The organizational culture also needs to move from rewarding *problem-solving* behaviors to rewarding problem prevention. This means including employees in a more proactive, collaborative approach that considers what could go wrong, how to prevent problems, and developing contingency plans should surprises occur. Today's information workers may actually know more about how to do their jobs than their managers do.

Shifting Beliefs and Attitudes

The shift to coach-based management requires examination of the beliefs, attitudes, skills, and habits we hold about managing. Making the following shifts will foster becoming an effective coach-based manager:

- Focus on the process, not just on the outcomes.

- Include everyone necessary to implement plans and decisions and solve problems.

- Adopt a management style that includes asking, listening and making requests.

- Share information, expectations and all relevant information that could be useful in getting others to fully commit to achieving the accountabilities.

Making the shift to coach-based management means managers must become:

- Accessible to the worker.

- Able to balance the focus on individual relationships with the accomplishment of tasks and results.

- Patient—be a coach instead of telling, fixing, and directing.

- Generous with praise and positive reinforcement.

- Understanding and supportive.

- A highly skilled listener.

- Concerned about fully developing the workers' talents.

- Willing to develop the skills necessary to turn good people into Top Talent.

The Changing Role of the Manager

Coach-based management results in a dramatic shift in the role of the manager or supervisor and may result in the question, "What do I do with this additional free time?" Figures 6.1 and 6.2 from The Leadership Development Process™, covered in Chapter Five, illustrate the roles and use of time before (figure 6.1) and after (figure 6.2) the shift to coach-based management.

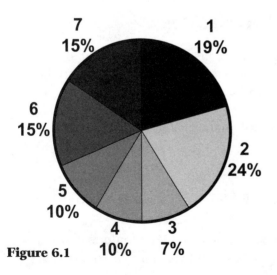

1. Directing Floor Activity
2. Production Reports
3. Miscellaneous
4. Trouble-shooting
5. Coaching & Training
6. Special Projects
7. Scheduling

Figure 6.1

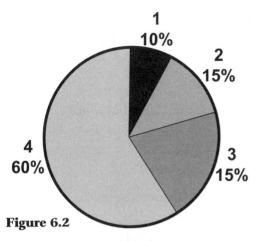

1. Budgeting
2. Management Responsibilities: Monitoring Overall Group Performance
3. Special Projects
4. Coaching and Training

Figure 6.2

Figure 6.1 illustrates that a typical manager spends as little as 10% of his or her time coaching and training. The majority of the time (53%) is consumed by directing work, trouble shooting, and generating production reports.

Figure 6.2 illustrates a redistribution of time to provide 60% for coaching and training by implementing a coach approach. Note the absence of time spent in trouble–shooting, which workers could perform with coaching from the manager. Workers can also absorb the scheduling and production reporting with the manager monitoring overall work group performance. Now there is additional time (10%) available for budgeting, which many managers claim they rarely have sufficient time to address.

A Coach Approach

A coach approach is a trust-based process intended to increase the effectiveness of the person being coached while maintaining his/her self-esteem. There are at least eight elements of a coach approach:

1. Considers Workers' Needs

A coach-based manager must maintain attention to all of the accountabilities previously mentioned while considering the five basic needs of every functional human being:

1. To be seen and acknowledged.

2. To be heard and receive response.

3. To feel respected and valued for making a unique contribution.

4. To feel safe and secure, physically and emotionally.

5. To feel included and have a sense of belonging and identity.

2. Shifts from Traditional Supervisory Techniques

A coach approach shifts away from traditional supervisory techniques, which often are based on lack of trust and a belief that workers have to be closely supervised in order to perform. A coach approach:

- Creates a trusting and collaborative environment in which personal development and performance improvement can occur.

- Involves respectful conversation that focuses on the person being coached.

- Encourages a positive style of relating that can be utilized anywhere, anytime.

- Provides a means for people to achieve extraordinary performance.

- Promotes reflection, self-discovery, and openness to taking more effective action.

3. Is Not Just for Problem People

Coaching is not just for problem people anymore. When I began my formal coach training in 1993, most coaches were hired to resolve performance problems, particularly corporate and executive coaches. When someone had a coach, it often implied failure; the person was being coached as a final opportunity to shape up or move on.

The primary focus of coaching today, and the primary work I do with The Effectiveness Coach® Approach, is turning good people into Top Talent. The emphasis is on optimizing capabilities to fully develop essential skills that maximize results. Most often, external coaching is provided for top performers with highly valued growth potential.

4. Focuses on Strengths

The coach approach allows workers to fully utilize their strengths by taking ownership of goals, making decisions, establishing action plans, and developing the commitment to implement them. With trust as the foundation, a coaching approach means workers become more self-monitoring, deciding how to handle problems at their level, including decisions about how to best accomplish the goals.

5. Doesn't Offer "Constructive Criticism"

Constructive criticism is truly a contradiction in terms. How can being critical also be constructive? It's more often destructive. Most people interpret criticism in any form as a personal attack that lowers self-esteem. In fact, critical people often suffer from low self- esteem and may resort to criticism in a futile effort to build themselves up. Furthermore, criticism usually focuses on the past rather than on the present or future and considers the problem more than the solution.

6. Addresses the Gap

An effective coach approach requires an agreement about the need to improve, to become better or different. Within my external coaching relationships, I begin by establishing agreement on the "gap" between where the client is and where he or she wants to be. This is often referred to as gap coaching. For an internal coach, such as a worker's manager or supervisor, the gap could be about performance improvement.

7. Models Integrity

The highly effective coach-based manager models integrity and high standards for others, continuously builds trust, and works toward establishing higher levels of responsibility and accountability.

8. Commits to Mastery

In addition to the skills mentioned in Key Five, Mastering the Essential Skills, adopting a coach approach requires specific coaching proficiencies and a high level of willingness and commitment to master them.

Performance Feedback

An effective coach-based manager will be highly skilled in delivering performance feedback, one of the most effective forms of coaching. Managers often overlook the need to provide reinforcement for a job well done. Top Talent welcomes feedback. It's important to acknowledge the contribution good people make on a regular basis and to recognize the need to feel appreciated. Positive feedback and encouragement contributes to keeping employees fully engaged.

Feedback Preparation Questions

When problems in performance require feedback, thoughtful preparation by the manager is required. Use these questions to prepare for a performance feedback coaching session.

1. What are the indicators of a performance gap?

2. How urgent or important is it to close the performance gap; is it mission critical or is there ample time to work out the issues?

3. What are the consequences for each of us in achieving or not achieving the established performance goals?

4. What specific skills are missing and may need to be developed?

5. What behaviors are inappropriate in this role, and how can I assist in modifying them?

6. What, if any, values and ethical issues are involved in this situation?

7. How have I contributed in some way to hinder this individual's performance?

8. What system or procedures may be limiting the results, and what actions can I take to remove them or reduce their impact on effective performance?

9. Where is this individual on the learning curve and experience in this job?

10. What factors could be causing a temporary setback and adversely affecting the worker's commitment or motivation?

11. What is my level of willingness to engage in a collaborative search for solutions and to let this worker's opinions and input influence me?

12. What assistance am I prepared to provide that could enhance the individual's willingness and ability to take appropriate actions? How effectively have I modeled the desired actions and behaviors?

13. What are my beliefs about this person's potential and how invested am I in this individual's success?

14. How can I assure that I am able to communicate in an unconditionally constructive manner?

15. Who else on our team could provide useful insights into this situation and collaborate with the worker and me?

Positive Performance Process

The following questions can be used to effectively address a performance issue. I call this a **Positive Performance Process**:

1. *What expectations and results have the individual and his or her manager agreed upon?* There must be agreement on the intended results, or there is no basis for a performance discussion. If necessary, establish the agreement on results initially and revisit periodically. For example, if an individual and his or her manager agree that a specific number of units will be produced each week, that number can be revisited periodically to revise the expectation in accordance with changing needs.

2. *What are the actual results?* Review the actual output in the same terms as was agreed upon.

3. *What is the gap between #1 and #2?* With agreement on the expectations and the actual accomplishment, it is now time to agree that there is gap. Manager and worker now agree that the number of units agreed to and expected was more than what is currently being produced.

4. *How important is it for us to close that gap?* Before moving on, establish that the gap is unacceptable and must be addressed. You can then move to the solution step, step 5 in the process. Here is where personal accountability comes into the picture; unless an individual agrees to be accountable for his or her performance based on steps one through three, lasting change will be unlikely.

5. *Beginning incrementally, what actions steps can we take to close this gap? By when can we close it?* With agreement on all four of the previous steps, it is now time to agree on what exactly will be done to raise performance levels to achieve the expected level agreed to in the first step. I frequently suggest that managers illustrate these steps. Two parallel lines can represent steps 1 and 2. The space between them is step 3. Step 5 can be illustrated as a stair step going from the lower line step 2 up to the upper line step 1.

I frequently suggest that managers illustrate these steps. Two parallel lines can represent steps 1 and 2. The space between them is step 3. Step 5 can be illustrated as a stair step going from the lower line step 2 up to the upper line step 1 as illustrated here:

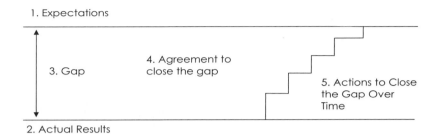

1. Expectations

3. Gap

4. Agreement to close the gap

5. Actions to Close the Gap Over Time

2. Actual Results

Based on the answers to these questions and the results of the performance coaching session, the manager will most likely become an observer, monitoring progress. However, it is essential that the manager maintain the same trust-based relationship and continue to treat the employee respectfully and optimistically during the agreed upon improvement period.

Evaluating the Feedback Experience

The quality of the feedback experience can be evaluated by asking these 10 questions:

1. Did I stimulate learning and inspire positive action?

2. Was feedback delivered in the present rather than at a time disconnected from the event or issue?

3. Did I intend to be helpful rather than to manipulate, coerce, or control?

4. Was feedback delivered in a positive, non-judgmental manner?

5. Was I compassionate and understanding while remaining authentic and candid?

6. Did I present observations rather than implications of negative motives or attitudes?

7. Did I enhance self-esteem, both the person receiving the feedback and mine?

8. Did the feedback process build trust or damage it?

9. Is the other person more committed to personal accountability than before?

10. Did I learn something about my leadership beliefs, skills, style, and attitudes?

Dialogue Skills of the Masterful Coach

Dialogue is another skill of the masterful coach and essential for the coach-based manager. Two-way, open-ended interaction balances speaking with listening for the purpose of creating mutual understanding, mutual meaning, and mutual respect.

Dialogue skills create another major challenge for the boss-oriented manager because he or she must be willing to shift from one-way communication and give up reliance on simply telling without listening. Making this shift is easier with an attitude that coaching is a form of learning and dialogue enhances learning.

Enhancing Learning Through Dialogue

Dialogue is a highly effective form of learning when the following skills and attitudes are present in the process:

- Open disclosure with no hidden agendas

- Sharing points of view truthfully with no withholding

- Valuing and respecting others' view points without judging

- Questioning for clarity rather than interrogating

- Listening to fully understand rather than to seek points of disagreement

You can enhance the effectiveness of your dialogue skills by using questions phrased to invite a personal response. Routinely include in your daily interaction with others one or more of the following eight questions adapted from the book *Enlightened Leadership* mentioned in the introduction:

1. In your opinion, what is the best approach to take in this situation?

2. How would you go about resolving this issue?

3. What do you think about the plan under consideration?

4. How could we improve on this idea?

5. If this were solely your decision, what would you do?

6. What do you consider our highest priority at the moment?

7. What else do we need to consider before going forward?

8. What has been overlooked or left out?

Benefits of Questions

Using questions enhances the learning process for many reasons. Listening to others' answers demonstrates respect and builds self-esteem by helping them to discover their own answers. You'll find that questions clarify the coachee's purpose and create alignment without directing. Questions also encourage greater learning by stimulating others' thinking and reframing situations to refocus attention toward the future.

Coached-Based Learning

Ideally, a coaching process will go beyond addressing performance gaps or problems to include fully developing personal skills. With a coach-based approach, learning becomes a personally customized trust-based relationship that increases an individual's capacity to apply what they have learned.

In Key Five, I discussed mastery of essential skills, The Cycle of Mastery™, and the importance of tying learning to measurable outcomes and business results. Figure 6.1 illustrates how coaching drives The Cycle of Mastery™ by assuring the connection with all of the components of the process.

A coach-based manager will assure that awareness occurs in the first step in the cycle and that a discovery is made in the second step. The coach is the essential element required to move the learning process along through application to accountability. For example, how often has reading books resulted in application of the books' discoveries? Many readers never get beyond awareness.

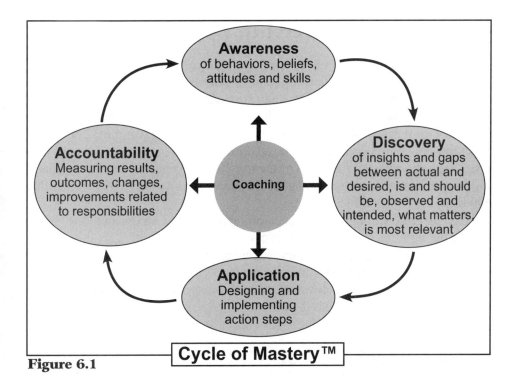

Figure 6.1

Mastery requires that the application of the learning produce results related to the accountabilities of the individual learner. How much do we really learn apart from what will be measured and for which we are accountable? At this point, the cycle repeats itself and continues until mastery is achieved.

Executive Coaching for Visionary Leaders

A recent survey of 100 senior executives released by Right Management Consultants found that coaching strategies have a measurable impact on return on investment—how much return was realized for the cost of the coaching provided. Senior executives report better relationships with their direct reports, supervisors, and peers, improved teamwork and greater job satisfaction. The organizational benefits include cost containment, less conflict management, productivity improvements, better relationships with the boss, team, or peers, and in some cases, retention of the executive.

Coaching for Leadership Development

The evidence is mounting in favor of professional coaching, particularly for executives in a leadership development or succession planning process. The 2003 Top Companies for Leaders Study conducted by Hewitt Associates found that companies with stronger leadership practices outperformed their industry peers in long-term measures of both financial growth and return. The use of executive coaching was a key factor separating the top companies from the others. The study revealed that 47% of the top 20 companies for leaders regularly assign coaches to their high-potential employees, while only 10% of the other 300 firms surveyed did so.

Executive coaching has also become recognized as an essential tool in reducing the timeline to achieve the level of proficiency required by the increasing demands of twenty-first century leaders and workers. We can conclude that coaching provides a powerful tool to accelerate performance and is critical to an organization's success. However, as with many strategic initiatives, coaching must begin at the top with the executive team.

Virtual Coaching For All Employees

With web-based technology it is now possible to provide a cost and time effective coach-based learning and development process to unlimited numbers of employees. Virtual coaching removes many of the barriers to providing the benefits of coaching to all key employees. The Effectiveness Coach® Approach, available from the Talent management Institute, includes an online component that replicates up to 80 percent of the process of personal coaching at a fraction of the cost with 24/7 access.

The ideal virtual coaching process includes assessments, 360-degree feedback, interactive learning, goal setting and personalized activities to achieve each individual's specific development objectives. I recommend a virtual coaching process as a systematic, structure approach to implementing a coach-based (development) process coordinated by HR or the training department. Even when performance coaching by the manager is the solution, a virtual coaching process can provide the learning and skill development required to develop essential, non-technical skills. When combined with personal coaching, the virtual component increases the results and benefits possible in less time.

Key Points

➤ Knowledge workers who expect to achieve personal fulfillment on the job want to be mentored and coached to fully develop their talents.

➤ Highly developed mentoring and coaching skills, particularly listening and giving and receiving feedback, have become essential elements for turning good people into Top Talent.

➤ Managers see themselves as responsible for outcomes, yet they are ill-equipped when it comes to knowing the best ways to achieve the desired result with today's worker.

➤ The following are five managerial challenges or key accountabilities of the job of manager.

1. To improve one's personal performance and results

2. To effectively manage both human and physical assets

3. To ensure that the work atmosphere is cooperative, non-threatening, and supportive

4. To be seen as a leader by all employees

5. To develop a management style that is participatory, open, flexible, and inclusive

➤ The common thread throughout these managerial accountabilities is the consideration of the human (intrinsic) side of the equation, not just the results (extrinsic) or the procedures and rules (systemic) to follow to achieve them.

➤ Recent surveys indicate organizations do not give themselves high marks at developing leaders. More than 70% reported their supervisors and managers do not have the skills to develop the capabilities of their direct reports.

➤ The shift to coach-based management begins with the premise that we must have an abiding faith and trust in people's desire to be great. The most effective coaching comes about when people ask to be coached.

➤ The organizational culture may also need to shift to rewarding problem-prevention behaviors rather than problem-solving behaviors.

➤ With trust as the foundation, a coach-based management approach means workers become more self-monitoring, deciding how to handle problems at their level, including decisions about how best to accomplish goals.

➤ The coach-based management approach focuses on five steps:

   1. Establishing a safe environment

   2. Sharing responsibility for creating dialogue

   3. Providing specific feedback

   4. Creating awareness that can lead to positive action

   5. Leveraging strengths

➤ Becoming an effective coach will be a stretch for many managers, requiring a major shift from being an autocratic boss or dictatorial supervisor.

➤ A coach approach is a shift from traditional supervisory techniques, which often are based on lack of trust and a belief that workers have to be closely supervised in order to perform.

➤ Coaching is not only for problem people anymore. Most often organizations provide external coaching for top performers whose growth potential they value highly.

➤ Coaching has become recognized as an essential tool to reduce the timeline to achieve the level of proficiency required by the increasing demands of twenty-first century leaders and workers.

➤ Ideally, executives can expect the relationship with a masterful coach to be transformational.

➤ A state-of-the-art on-line virtual coaching process can provide unlimited coaching capacity for increasing leadership, management, and sales effectiveness along with balancing work and life, and creating the dream job. Thus, there is little reason left for anyone not to receive the benefits of a coaching process.

Questions to Ponder

1. How important is it for your managers to make the shift to coaching-based management?

2. To what extent are managers in your organization achieving the five accountabilities common to all management positions?

3. How well are managers using a coach-based approach to maximize their contribution?

4. How many of the benefits of executive coaching are important to you?

5. How urgent is it to get everyone fully engaged and willing to be accountable for results?

TABS Action Plan

T .   What was the main **thing** you got from this key?

A .   What **action** are you willing to take?

B .   What **benefit** do you expect to get from it?

S .   What is the **single step** you will take to **get started** within 48 hours?

Assignments

- Select from the ten reasons to adopt coach-based management, those that relate to your organization.

- Discuss with your management team what it would take to make the shift to coach-based managing.

- Determine how effectively your managers are practicing feedback and dialogue.

- Assess the level of manager contribution related to the five accountabilities and challenges.

- Consider a pilot on-line coaching process for those being groomed for leadership.

KEY  SEVEN

TALENT MANAGEMENT:

MAXIMIZING ENGAGEMENT, RETENTION AND UTILIZATION

"No company can expect to beat the competition unless it has the best human capital and promotes these people to pivotal positions. Meeting medium and long-term milestones greatly depends on having a pipeline of promising and promotable employees. You need to assess them today, and decide what each employee needs to do to become ready to take on larger responsibilities. Nothing is more important to an organization's competitive edge."

- Lawrence Bossidy, Chairman, Honeywell Corp. and co-author of
Execution: The Discipline of Getting Things Done

TALENT MANAGEMENT

Imagine . . . the positive impact on your bottom line with a workforce of fully engaged Top Talent executing your organization's strategy . . . every day!

What Exactly is Talent Management?

Just a few years ago, an Internet search for "talent management" would yield a sizable list of organizations that manage performers such as actors and musicians, otherwise known as "talent." Today, entering the search term "talent management" into Google.com yields over 2,600,000 results. Most of the top ten listings had something to do with employees rather than entertainers.

In the context of turning good people into Top Talent—the title of this book, after all—the term "talent management" refers to a pool of leaders and key professional and technical employees who, on average, comprise only about 15% of the workforce. According to Towers Perrin 2005 *Talent Management: The State of the Art: A TP Track Research Report* survey of more that 250 executives, 86% considered senior leadership groups as "talent," 82% included those with leadership potential in midlevel jobs, 76% included key contributors/technical experts, and 48% included those with leadership potential in entry-level positions.

Why the Focus on Talent Management?

According to the 2005 *TP Track* report, the increased attention being given to talent management is caused by factors like a "changing competitive landscape, requiring new skills, knowledge and behaviors" and an "increased focus on customer satisfaction and retention." In the globally competitive business environment of the 21st century, the surge of retiring executive talent, predictions of inadequate workforce numbers, and failure to have adequate succession plans puts organizations at risk.

Top Talent Performance

Research consistently shows that Top Talent exceeds the performance of average workers by at least 25%. In some cases, the differential was 100%! The Top Talent differential includes:

- Higher productivity

- Higher sales volume

- Better customer service, retention, and loyalty

- Problem solving, not problem creating

- Making things happen—getting it done!

A stable workforce of Top Talent has become the primary competitive advantage for companies that want to maximize results. As Jim Collins tells us in his book, *Good to Great*, you must have the right people on the bus and in the right seats—even before you decide where the bus is going. Therefore, you must implement a process that matches talent with the job in order to get the right people in the right jobs in the first place.

Effective Talent Management

The Turning Good People Into Top Talent Process™ directly supports the strategic goals and objectives of the organization. The process aligns human resource initiatives to overall business strategy. Effective talent management can only be accomplished when the organizational culture is ready to support it through alignment, vision, credibility, and empowerment.

Alignment

The leadership of the organization must understand, agree on, and commit to purpose, values, vision, goals, procedures, and roles in order to convey this information to the workforce:

- Purpose – Why, other than profit, are we here?

- Vision – Where are we going?

- Shared Values – How do we behave and operate?

- Goals – What do we intend to accomplish in the next 3-10 years?

- Roles – Who will do what?

- Procedures – How will we do it?

These strategic elements were covered in Chapter Two: Organizational Vitality. In that chapter, I illustrate how to measure the elements and determine the degree of alignment.

Credibility

Top Talent are attracted to a trusted employer of choice, which means:

- Doing what matters most to customers and employees.

- Consistently delivering value.

- Continuously practicing trust-building behaviors.

- Living the values that allow trust-building.

Empowerment

Leaders who consistently empower workers do so by encouraging acts of shared leadership while managing the talent development process. Leaders at all levels must become coach-based managers, as we discussed in Chapter Six. Coach-based mangers promote mastery of essential skills by facilitating continuous learning and develop high levels of emotional intelligence.

Alignment, credibility, and empowerment create a culture of personal accountability, the basis for role awareness, commitment, and action. I call this an A.C.E.™ Organization. Balance among these three elements creates the window that makes effective talent management possible, illustrated in Figure 7.1 by the triangle in the center of this diagram.

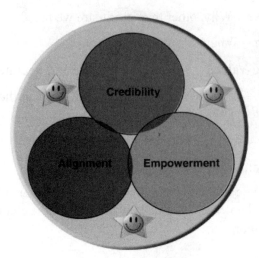

Figure 7.1

The A.C.E.™ Organization
A Responsibility-Based Culture
and Values Driven Workplace

Getting to the heart of engagement, retention, and utilization requires a strategic approach to talent management.

Is Turnover the Real Problem?

Many executives and senior managers continue to rank employee turnover as one of the greatest challenges they face. A Harvard University study concludes that 80% of employee turnover can be traced back to mistakes made during the hiring or promotion process. Clearly, an effective hiring process can improve retention.

Good People

Effective talent management identifies "good people," newly hired workers as well as those already a part of the organization, who can become Top Talent. My research reveals that organizations frequently have a mismatch or poor "fit" between people and jobs...not really untalented people. The relevance of mismatching talent is further validated in a study of approximately 300,000 subjects, published in *Harvard Business Review*, which revealed that the only statistically significant difference in job performance was in the area of "job match." The study concluded that success hinges solely on an employee's fit with the job, not experience, education, or other accepted factors.

Jobseeker Research

Recent research conducted by TTI Ltd. of online job seekers reveals some surprising trends. The research concluded workers are looking for meaningful employment, a place where they can fully utilize their skills to make a difference and be valued and appreciated. They are looking for a good job fit.

- 65% are leaving their current employer for reasons other than the "Big 4" (salary, benefits, working conditions, and quality of supervision).

- 92% said it's more important to find the *right* job than *any* job.

- 40% will job hunt as long as it takes to find the right job.

- 40% have applied for 51 or more jobs.

Best Practices for Hiring

Best practices for hiring, illustrated by Figure 7.2 are a component of the Turning Good People Into Top Talent Process™ (This is illustrated in Figure 7.3, later in this chapter.) An effective hiring process is designed to attract a flow of candidates best suited for the job, screen for good people who have the potential to become Top Talent, select those whose talents best match the requirements of the job, and integrate them into the organization.

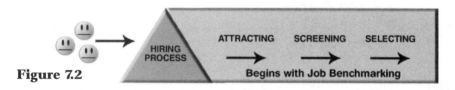

Figure 7.2

Job Benchmarking

The basis for an effective hiring process is job benchmarking, which assures you'll get the right person in the right job, because the process takes into account the unique requirements of this job within your organization. This process begins with identifying the accountabilities of the job, defined as that which it was designed to accomplish. This is more than a job description, which is often just a list of tasks and duties.

When I facilitate a benchmarking session with key stakeholders, I frequently ask, "What are the top three reasons the job exists? If the job could talk, what would it tell us about what's required to do it well…to accomplish the accountabilities?"

When you are clear about the technical skills, experience, and background, you must also determine the measurable talents required for superior performance as discussed in Chapter Five, such as:

- *Behaviors* like versatility, competitiveness, analysis of data, and organized workspace that determine how we behave in the workplace.

- *Motivators*: rewards that determine why we do what we do in the job, including opportunities to make a difference, achieve measurable results, acquire knowledge, and utilize skills.

- *Attributes*: capacities that determine if the individual can and will do the job and how well, such as personal accountability, self-starting ability, conceptual thinking, and resiliency.

The Turning Good People Into Top Talent Process™ includes the TriMetrix™ assessment system to measure these three areas.

Recent research findings indicate the relationship between specific attributes and job success. For example, the skill of self-management consistently placed in the top seven personal attributes considered essential to success by stakeholders who provided input to job benchmarking.

Here is a sample of titles of benchmarked positions with the number of stakeholder respondents in the study and the percent of them who considered self-management a top seven priority:

- CEO: 81% of 5,107 respondents

- Technical Staff: 96% of 3,452 respondents

- Customer Service: 100% of 1,500 respondents

- Supervisors: 94% of 6,385 respondents

- Outside Sales: 78% of 4,291 respondents

Further research is already beginning to illustrate the importance of determining an individual's strengths in skills that are not essential to a particular job. People tend to focus on and utilize their strengths. Measuring these skills can prevent disaster since their over-use can be detrimental to performance. Think of the benefits to the individual and the organization of focusing on developing and fully utilizing what really matters most on the job. These findings provide strong evidence of the importance of identifying both the essential and non-essential skills of the job.

Prescreening

A recent study on hiring found that 95% of applicants exaggerate to get a job, and that most hiring decisions are made based on intuition during the first few minutes of the interview. Efficient and effective prescreening must be utilized to process job candidates so that only those who have real potential for good job fit advance to the assessment and selection phase of the process.

Prescreening can include job specific criteria such as education, technical skills, experience, expected salary, etc., and should always include screening for counterproductive behaviors. I recommend the use of an assessment that can identify risks related to issues such as anger management, attitude toward authority, safety, sexual harassment, theft, and drug use. It's extremely important to include appropriate prescreening with each position, since one bad hire can have devastating consequences on the safety and stability of your workforce.

Screening and Selection

Effective applicant screening includes a fully validated assessment process incorporating measurement of the essential skills required for top performance in the job. This provides the basis for up to one-third of the decision. An additional one-third of the decision is based on the specific technical skills required along with the relevant experience. The final one-third should include the interview results and determining the candidate's fit with the organization's culture. The results of assessments used in the hiring process become the basis for the individual's development plan and may actually begin during onboarding.

A Case Study

Companies that use the TriMetrix™ assessment system, a component of the Turning Good People Into Top Talent Process, as a part of their hiring process see an average increase of more than five times in successful hires. The system begins with a job benchmark and then measures why, how, and what an individual can contribute to the job.

Last year, a Houston-based homebuilding firm was faced with increasing turnover and decreasing sales. Maintaining market share, stabilizing productivity, and the survival of the company were all in question. The company simply had to find a way to stop the churn in its sales force. The root of the problem was poor hiring decisions caused by a lack of understanding of the sales job. Hiring managers did not know what talents were necessary for success.

Implementation of the solution began by benchmarking the sales job by bringing all the stakeholders together to analyze the job. Based on the job benchmark, a set of interview questions were developed that addressed the specific talents the job required. By combining the interview questions with assessment of the candidates' talents, potential superior performers where identified.

The homebuilding firm only hired potentially Top Talent. In less than a year, turnover has decreased by 75%, and sales have increased by 50%. The company has now extended the hiring system into its homebuilding division and benchmarked every executive position including CEO. The company reports widespread organizational improvement to this day.

Onboarding

Identifying good people is a good start, but alone, it is simply not enough. How do you make sure you can keep the talent you have acquired? Challenges with engagement, utilization, and retention indicate much larger issues within an organization.

For both the newly hired worker and those currently employed with the organization, effective onboarding is critical for early engagement and success in the job. Top Talent are "doers" who require a quick start, clear expectations, and frequent performance feedback. The same TTI Ltd. Study that identified jobseeker trends uncovered these attitudes and preferences of what they would like to see happen the first day of a new job:

- No paperwork! Provide an opportunity to complete forms prior to the first work day.

- Most workers want to make a fast start and feel productive and valued from the beginning.

- Give them the opportunity to meet with those supervisors who will be responsible for evaluating their performance.

- Arrange for them to meet the company's top executives.

Further, the survey respondents said that for the first 90 days on the job, they want to be told and shown what is expected of them, to feel free to ask questions and observe, and to know where to go for information. They want to be coached and mentored.

Assure Effective Engagement

Put yourself in the following situation. As CEO of ZYX Corp., an emerging leader in the software development field, your strategy is to grow the organization through innovative products, customer-centric marketing, and responsive customer service and support. The company has hired good people with the skills, experience, and knowledge to excel in their jobs.

Even though the company is making rapid progress, you have noticed more time and resources being spent on hiring new people. Upon investigation, you discover that your best people are leaving. In fact, in the past three months, many of your star performers have left to work for your competitors.

In your investigation, you discover Don, a talented technician, has just quit. Don was hired seven months ago for his experience and expert technical skills. Notes from his exit interview indicate that, almost from the beginning, Don felt disconnected and uncomfortable. He stated that assignments and expectations were unclear. He was frequently not informed of team meetings. Don's direct supervisor often publicly criticized team members when deadlines were missed or problems occurred. Don wondered when he would become a target and grew distrustful of his supervisor.

After several months of employment, Don was still not involved in establishing the objectives for projects he worked on while other team members were often asked for input when problems came up. Don was rarely given the opportunity to express his opinions or to contribute toward solutions. Finally, after seven months, his initial excitement was gone, and he felt unappreciated and underutilized. He began to conclude that there was little or no opportunity to make a difference and apply his specialized knowledge, skills, and talents

Don left for a better opportunity, becoming another retention statistic.

What Workers Really Want

A Gallup Organization study of over 100,000 employees from more than 2500 business units found that what encourages retention of top performers is managers who recognize workers' talents and strengths and encourage their development. Here is what mattered most to employees:

- Understanding why I am here and what is expected of me in my job

- Being given the resources and materials that I need to do my job right

- Getting the opportunity to engage in what I do best just about every day

- Having a manager or co-workers who relate to and care about me as a person, not just as a worker

- Expressing opinions that matter

- Receiving recognition for doing a job well

- Having someone at work who encourages and supports me personally

- Getting coaching, constructive feedback, and support from my manager

- Experiencing positive two-way communication with my manager

- Feeling valued and being paid according to my worth

As this list reveals, the manager has a unique opportunity to create or at least co-create the environment most conducive to success. One of the best ways to accomplish this is to determine the degree to which work expectations are being met. Unspoken, unmet expectations in the workplace can lead to job frustration, substandard performance, decreased job commitment, and high turnover.

Continuous Development

Effective talent management continues beyond getting the right person in the right job. Maximizing engagement, utilization, and retention requires a process that includes

- Coaching and mentoring

- Continuous learning

- Performance management

- Innovation and idea management

- Work expectations

- Compensation and benefits management

- Career path / succession planning

For both newly hired individuals and the currently employed, information gained in the selection process becomes the basis for a personalized development plan. Benchmarking key positions and matching the worker's talents with the job requirements provides a solid foundation for a developmental program by identifying gaps between job requirements and each individual's talents. Superior performance can be assured by building the essential skills required for the specific job.

The results of the benchmark also provides input to a 360° multiple rater survey to assess the application of each worker's talents 60 to 90 days after placing the worker in the job. This type of feedback on performance becomes the basis for continuous refinement of the individual's development plan.

Succession Planning

Research on putting "the right person with the right talent in the right position" reveals that workers promoted from within an organization tend to stay with the organization and become top performers at a much higher percentage than those brought in from outside. However, organizational growth and change places increased demands and expectations on those in key positions. People assume or are appointed to positions to "get the job done" without much thought about human resource planning. As more capability and capacity is required, talented people in key positions may no longer have the talent required to achieve the new demands. When current positions open up because of retirement, promotion, or a variety of unexpected reasons, succession issues arise.

To effectively address these issues, an objective third party from outside the organization must systematically define the scope of the position and its talent requirements. Often, an additional issue arises of how to communicate the gap (degree of fit) between the position requirements and the position holder's talent. The following process, developed by my colleague Dr. Shayne Tracy of Newhouse Partners, provides a rational approach to managing this succession challenge.

Organization Chart and Position Review

The process begins by reviewing the organization chart to familiarize yourself with the overall structure and titles in the organization and the general job culture.

To ensure the right person with the right talent is in the right position requires a position review. This review involves the following eight assumptions and activities:

1. The position description defining the responsibilities, accountabilities and core tasks for a position must be clearly identified in relation to other positions.

2. Inherent in a position is its Talent DNA™[1]* which is made up of behaviors, values and attitudes, soft skill attributes, and technical skills.

3. It is important to benchmark a position to identify the top Talent DNA requirements (behaviors, values and attitudes, essential personal and technical skills requirement required by the job).

4. After benchmarking the position, the position holder is assessed to determine the "degree of fit" between the position Talent DNA required and the Talent DNA of the position holder.

5. In an executive team where the position holders are peers, a low degree of fit between position and position holder will have a significant dysfunctional effect within the team and within the company.

6. Where the degree of fit is below acceptable levels, it may be necessary to remove the position holder from the position.

7. Personal and professional development including personal coaching can be provided to work on closing the gaps between the job requirements and the position holder's talents.

8. To assure maximum performance on an executive team, we recommend precision talent mapping of the entire team.

---

1 * Talent DNA is a trademark of Newhouse Partners.

Position Holder Review

Next is the position holder review which involves the following seven steps.

1. The position holder completes a Position Description Questionnaire (PDQ) to provide details on how they perceive their position.

2. The position holder is assessed to identify their Talent DNA (behaviors, values and attitudes and soft skill attributes).

3. The position holder is interviewed to validate their perception of the position against the Position Description Questionnaire.

4. A 360 multi-rater feedback survey is used to obtain data from the position holder and selected persons who interact with the position holder in the workplace.

5. The Talent Assessment is reviewed with the position holder.

6. Recommendations are made on the "degree of fit" between the position and the position holder.

7. Coaching is provided as required depending on the degree of fit.

Succession Planning Summary

Using a third party to provide objectivity with succession challenges is extremely beneficial. Through systematic position analysis and assessment, combined with position holder talent review and assessment, the organization can more effectively place the right people with the right talent in the right position.

Talent Management Summary

Effective talent management can only occur within a values-driven workforce and a culture of accountability. The Turning Good People Into Top Talent Process includes the following elements which are illustrated in Figure 7.3:

- Align HR practices with the business strategy.
- Benchmark all jobs essential to the execution of the strategy by involving key stakeholders in determining job accountabilities.

- Prescreen candidates (online is recommended to efficiently process high volume applicant flow).

- Establish interview questions based on the job benchmark.

- Conduct effective interviews using relevant questions.

- Use validated assessments to measure essential skills, behaviors, and attributes required for job success and compare these with the job benchmark.

- Select using the 1/3-1/3-1/3 principle.

- Include an onboarding process that assures early engagement.

- Practice coach-based management with routine measurement of job expectations and 360° feedback.

- Provide continuous skills development with the Effectiveness Coach® Approach including the Cycle of Mastery™ as discussed in Chapter Six.

- Establish systematic career path and succession planning.

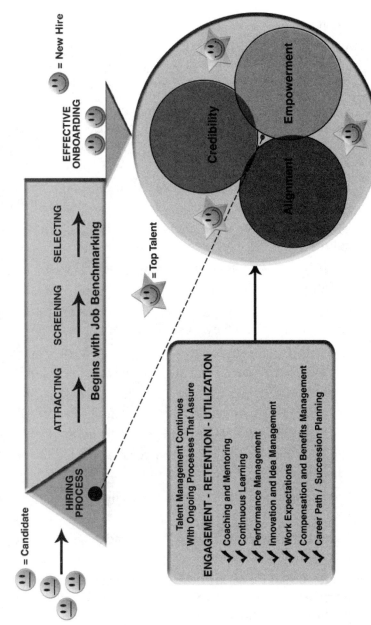

The Turning Good People into Top Talent Process™

Effective Talent Management requires an A.C.E.™ Organization

= Candidate

ATTRACTING   SCREENING   SELECTING

Begins with Job Benchmarking

EFFECTIVE ONBOARDING

= New Hire

HIRING PROCESS

= Top Talent

Talent Management Continues
With Ongoing Processes That Assure

ENGAGEMENT - RETENTION - UTILIZATION

✔ Coaching and Mentoring
✔ Continuous Learning
✔ Performance Management
✔ Innovation and Idea Management
✔ Work Expectations
✔ Compensation and Benefits Management
✔ Career Path / Succession Planning

Credibility

Empowerment

Alignment

The A.C.E.™ Organization
A Responsibility-Based Culture
and Values Driven Workplace

Figure 7.3

© Copyright 2005, Robert B. Moore, Effectiveness, Inc.

Key Points

- The term "talent management" refers to a pool of leaders and key professional and technical employees that, on average, comprise only about 15% of the workforce.

- Increased attention is being given to talent management because of the changing competitive landscape, requiring new skills, knowledge, and behaviors and an increased focus on customer satisfaction and retention.

- Research reveals that Top Talent exceeds the performance of average workers by at least 25% and in some cases 100%.

- Effective talent management requires a responsibility-based culture and a values-driven workforce.

- A strategic approach is needed to maximize engagement, retention and utilization.

- Current research indicates workers want meaningful employment where they can make a difference.

- A Harvard University study concludes that 80% of employee turnover can be traced to mistakes made during the hiring or promotion process.

- To maximize your competitive advantage, reduce costly turnover by placing the right person in the job the *first* time.

- Job benchmarking of highly leveragable positions is the basis for an effective hiring process.

- Specific personal attributes have been identified as necessary for job success.

- Prescreening assures only qualified candidates reach the interview stage.

- Up to 90% of the hiring decision is typically based on interviews, which have only 14% effectiveness as a predictor of future performance.

- Use validated assessments to measure and match workers' strengths with the requirements of the job. It is also important to note any non-essential skills that may be a candidate's strengths since use of these can interfere with performance.

- Effective onboarding is essential to early engagement and retention of Top Talent.

- Top Talent values feedback and a development plan.

- In most organizations, there is often a mismatch or poor fit between people and jobs...not untalented people.

- Positions open up due to retirement, promotion, or a variety of unexpected reasons, creating succession issues that must be addressed.

- Using a third party to provide objectivity with succession challenges is extremely beneficial.

- Through systematic position and position holder analysis and assessment, the organization can more effectively place the right people with the right talent in the right positions.

Questions to Ponder

1. What would getting to the heart of engagement, retention, and utilization do for the execution of your organization's strategy?

2. Are you focused on turnover instead of making sure the right people are in the right job and becoming fully engaged?

3. What process do you have to efficiently incorporate (onboard) new employees into the organization?

4. How effective is your development plan for good people you expect to become Top Talent throughout your organization?

5. What succession plan or process is in place for key positions that are critical to the execution of your strategy?

TABS Action Plan

T. What was the main **thing** you got from this chapter?

A. What **action** are you willing to take?

B. What **benefit** do you expect to get from it?

S. What is the **single step** you will take to **get started** within 48 hours?

Assignments

- Select a key position and ask yourself the real reason the job exists. If the job could talk, what would it say about the talent required for superior performance?

- Meet with your management team to determine what it would take to fully execute your strategy and achieve the organization's priority goals. Is it engagement, retention, or utilization? Then, create a plan to implement the appropriate solution.

- Determine your most highly leveragable positions, those most critical to the execution of your strategy, and decide how you will assure that the right person with the right talent will be available at the right time.

In the next chapter, I will pull together the key points we have covered throughout this book.

CHAPTER EIGHT

REVIEW AND ACTION PLAN

"Genuine beginnings begin within us, even when they are brought to our attention by external circumstance."

- William Bridges,
Transition: The Personal Path Through Change

REVIEW AND ACTION PLAN

Winning companies have a strategy focused on achieving goals that include growth, customer satisfaction, and innovation. A strategy that includes talent management is the most effective way to address epidemic worker disengagement, high levels of employee turnover, and under-utilization of talent. Turning good people into Top Talent is the solution to costly challenges such as declining production, increased expenses, declining customer satisfaction, shrinking market share, and loss of revenue and profit.

The Turning Good People Into Top Talent Process™ includes an effective talent management process within an A.C.E.™ organization that solves engagement, retention, and utilization challenges. An A.C.E.™ organization has a responsibility-based culture and a values-driven workforce created through Alignment with purpose, vision and values, Credibility as a trusted employer of choice, and Empowerment by mastering essential leadership skills.

The following A.C.E.™ diagram (Figure 8.1) illustrates the three ACE elements fully developed and in balance creating the triangle, which is the entry point for good people to enter the organization to become Top Talent. The flow chart (8.2) illustrates the process of implementing the steps to Becoming an A.C.E.™ organization, a major component of the Turning Good People Into Top Talent Process™.

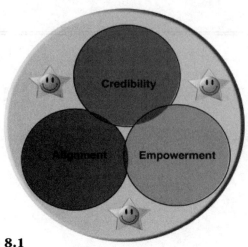

Figure 8.1

The A.C.E.™ Organization
A Responsibility-Based Culture
and Values Driven Workplace

Action Plan: Where to Begin

1. Assure readiness for a responsibility-based culture—Get the senior team aligned.

2. Benchmark the organization's vital signs—Assess the current culture.

3. Assess leadership competency—Measure gaps between current and desired levels.

4. Identify talent requirements—Effective talent management begins with benchmarking.

5. Engage a coach-based consultant to guide you on the journey—A competent professional resource can accelerate the process.

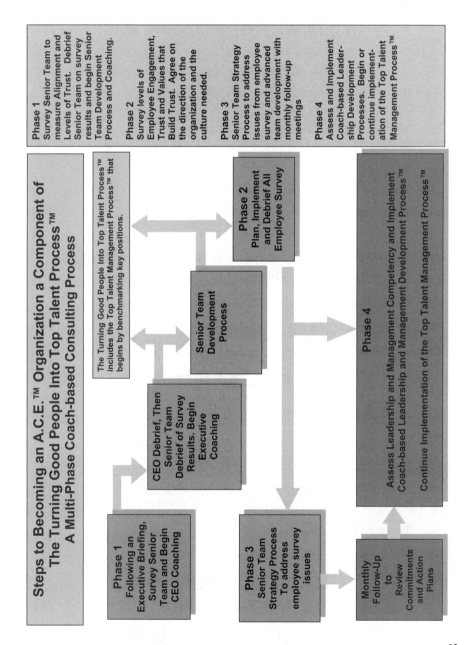

Steps to Becoming an A.C.E.™ Organization a Component of The Turning Good People Into Top Talent Process™ A Multi-Phase Coach-based Consulting Process

The Turning Good People Into Top Talent Process™ includes the Top Talent Management Process™ that begins by benchmarking key positions.

Phase 1
Following an Executive Briefing, Survey Senior Team and Begin CEO Coaching

CEO Debrief, Then Senior Team Debrief of Survey Results. Begin Executive Coaching

Senior Team Development Process

Phase 2
Plan, Implement and Debrief All Employee Survey

Phase 3
Senior Team Strategy Process To address employee survey issues

Monthly Follow-Up to Review Commitments and Action Plans

Phase 4
Assess Leadership and Management Competency and Implement Coach-based Leadership and Management Development Process™

Continue Implementation of the Top Talent Management Process™

Phase 1
Survey Senior Team to measure Alignment and Levels of Trust. Debrief Senior Team on survey results and begin Senior Team Development Process and Coaching.

Phase 2
Survey levels of Employee Engagement, Trust and Values that Build Trust. Agree on the direction of the organization and the culture needed.

Phase 3
Senior Team Strategy Process to address issues from employee survey and advanced team development with monthly follow-up meetings

Phase 4
Assess and Implement Coach-based Leadership Development Processes. Begin or continue implementation of the Top Talent Management Process™

Figure 8.2

"Imagine…the positive impact on your bottom line with a workforce of fully engaged Top Talent executing your organization's strategy…every day!"

Feel free to contact me for support in the execution of *your* strategy for turning good people into Top Talent!

Bob Moore, CMC®, MCC
The Top Talent Guru™

Phone: 813-286-7320 | 888-NOW EXCEL (669-3923)
Email: bob@effectiveness.com | Visit: www.toptalentguru.com

ABOUT THE AUTHOR
ROBERT B. MOORE, CMC, MCC
THE EFFECTIVENSS COACH© AND TOP TALENT GURU™

Bob Moore is an executive resource and talent management strategist supporting business leaders in the execution of their strategy by maximizing worker engagement, retention and full utilization of talent. His clients include executives and professionals who report exceptional outcomes with measurable results achieved by addressing their strategic talent management challenges.   Bob is a unique combination of

Experience
- CEO of Effectiveness, Inc, founder of The Talent Management Institute™, over four decades as an entrepreneur, business owner, industry leader and professional

Credentials
- The Effectiveness Coach® and Coach-based Consultant™ both a Certified Management Consultant—CMC® and Master Certified Coach—MCC

Expertise
- The Top Talent Guru™, expert presenter and author with over a quarter-century of active membership in the National Speakers Association.

Inspiration
- A unique combination of expertise and enthusiasm that both entertains and challenges in the boardroom or conference hall.

To book Bob Moore for your conference or an executive retreat call 813-286-7320 or 888-NOW EXCEL (669-3923) or email bob@effectiveness.com or visit www.toptalentguru.com

Learn more about the Effectiveness Coach ® Approach at www.theeffectivenesscoach.com

BIBLIOGRAPHY & REFERENCES

Blanchard, Kenneth H., et al. *Managing By Values*. San Francisco: Berrett-Koehler Publishers, 1997.

Bossidy, Larry, et al. *Execution: The Discipline of Getting Things Done*. New York: Crown Business, 2002.

Collins, Jim. *Good to Great*. New York: HarperCollins, 2001.

Drucker, Peter. *Peter Drucker on the Profession of Management*. Boston: Harvard Business Review Book, 2004.

Goleman, Daniel. *Primal Leadership*. Boston: Harvard Business School Press, 2002.

Katzenback, Jon R. and Douglas K. Smith. *Wisdom of Teams: Creating the High-Performance Organization*. New York: Harper Business, 1994.

Kennedy, Allan. *The End of Shareholder Value: Corporations at the Crossroads*. Cambridge: Perseus Publishing, 2000.

Lebow, Rob and Randy Spitzer. *Accountability: Freedom and Responsibility Without Control*. San Francisco: Berrett-Koehler, 2002.

Leonard, George Burr. *Mastery: The Keys to Success and Long-Term Fulfillment*. New York: Plume, 1992.

Naisbitt, John. *Megatrends.* New York: Warner Books, Inc., 1982.

Nalbantian, Haig, et al. *Play to Your Strengths: Managing Your Internal Labor Markets for Lasting Competitive Advantage.* New York: McGraw-Hill, 2003.

Oakley, Ed and Doug Krug. *Enlightened Leadership.* New York: Fireside, 1994.

Peters, Thomas J. and Robert H. Waterman, Jr. *In Search of Excellence.* New York: HarperCollins, 2004.

Reichheld, Frederick F. and W. Earl Sasser, Jr. *Zero Defections: Quality Comes to Service.* Boston: Harvard Business Review, 2000.

Senge, Peter. *The Fifth Discipline.* New York: Doubleday, 1990.

Stayer, Ralph. *How I Learned to Let My Workers Lead.* Boston: Harvard Business Review, 1990.

INDEX

RECOMMENDED READING FOR LEADERS

A Whole New Mind by Daniel Pink, H Penguin Group

Blink by Malcolm Gladwell, Little, Brown and Company

Blue Ocean Strategy by W. Chan Kim and Renee Mauborne, Harvard Business School Press

Clued In: How to Keep Customers Coming Back Again and Again by Lewis P. Carbone, Financial Times/Prentice Hall

Enlightened Leadership by Ed Oakley and Doug Krug, Fireside

Free Prize Inside by Seth Godin, Portfolio

Good to Great by Jim Collins, HarperBusiness

Guts!: Companies That Blow the Doors off Business-as-Usual by Jackie Freiberg and Kevin Freiberg, Currency

Leading Organizational Learning: Harnessing the Power of Knowledge by Marshall Goldsmith, Howard Morgan, Alexander J. Ogg, Niall Fitzgerald and Frances Hesselbein, Leader to Leader Institute

Leadership from the Inside Out by Kevin Cashman, TCLG

Leadership Is an Art by Max De Pree, Currency

Love 'Em or Lose 'Em by Beverly L. Kaye and Sharon Jordan-Evans, Berrett-Koehler

Management Challenges for the 21st Century by Peter Drucker, HarperBusiness

Masterful Coaching, Revised Edition by Robert Hargrove, Jossey-Bass

On Value and Values by Douglas K. Smith, Pearson Education

Purple Cow by Seth Godin, Portfolio

Results-Based Leadership by David Ulrich, Jack Zenger, and Norm Smallwood, Harvard Business School Press

Return on Customer by Don Peppers and Martha Rogers, Bantam Dell Pub Group

The 7 Habits of Highly Effective People by Stephen R. Covey, Simon & Schuster

The Feiner Points of Leadership by Michael Feiner, Warner Business Books

The Naked Corporation: How the Age of Transparency Will Revolutionize Business by Don Tapscott and David Ticoll, Free Press

The Purpose-Driven Life: What on Earth Am I Here For? by Rick Warren, Zondervan.

Winning by Jack and Suzy Welch, HarperCollins

What's Coming?

- A complete 6 CD audio version with reference guide of *Turning Good People Into Top Talent: Key Leadership Strategies for a Winning Company*

- The Top Talent Workshop Series of the Seven Keys

- The Top Talent Executive Symposium Series for corporate or sponsor groups

- Top Talent Keynote (30 to 90 minutes) for associations and corporate meetings

To receive advance notice of new products and services, call 813-286-7320 or 888-NOW-EXCEL (669-3923)

Or email bob@toptalentguru.com

Look us up for new postings, place orders, and make inquiries at www.toptalentbook.com and www.toptalentguru.com

We welcome the opportunity to serve you!

Bob Moore CMC, MCC

"Imagine...the positive impact on your bottom line with a workforce of fully engaged Top Talent executing your organization's strategy... every day!"

Check bookstores everywhere or order here.
Toll-Free: 1-888-669-3923
place secure online order at
www.toptalentbook.com

TURNING GOOD PEOPLE INTO TOP TALENT KEY LEADERSHIP STRATEGIES FOR A WINNING COMPANY	#	Total
Hardcover Book $24.95		
6 CD Audio Album with Reference Guide $249.00		
Shipping		
Order Total		

Shipping in US:
$5.00 for each book, $2.00 for each additional book.
$7.00 for each Audio Album, $2.00 for each additional item
Prices and shipping charges subject to change without notice.

Please Print

Name _____

Company_____

Ship To _____

City/State _____ Zip _____

Phone _____ Email (optional) _____

Effectiveness Press
P.O. Box 25936
Tampa, FL 33622
www.toptalentbook.com
Phone: 888-669-3923